Timeless Top 10 Travel Guides

TOKYO

Tokyo Top 10 Hotel, Shopping and Dining, Off – Road

Adventures, Events, Historical Landmarks, Nightlife, Top

Things to do and Much More!

By Tess Downey

Foreword

Tokyo is a place unlike any other that it has the eyes of the world transfixed in awe at the precision-like function, and progress of the most populated spot on Earth. Like a well-oiled machine, the thriving city metropolis operates at a pace that pulsates to a rhythmic beat in step with modernity. A forerunner in the realm of science and technology, the Land of Cherry Blossoms dares to imagine and continues to push new boundaries, and setting standards. Despite all this, Tokyo has been steadfast in keeping their heritage alive by celebrating traditions passed down by their ancestors. A modern city metropolis in every scope of the landscape, it is a culture rich in tradition charged to keeping these practices alive, in ways that not only celebrate their ancestors, but also their heritage.

The thriving and busy metropolis of Tokyo has been recognized as the forerunner in city cleanliness and maintenance with its litter-free roads and thoroughfares. It ranks first in the category of "city with the most helpful and accommodating locals" who are kindly and accommodating to strangers from other shores. It is host to some of the biggest and most successful international banks and companies. Internal fashion houses have called Tokyo their home away from home and have been a big part of the industry and trade affairs of the forward-moving state for a long time. Some of the best name brand ateliers and clothing franchises can be found here.

There is never a shortage of places to check out in this enthralling city. Whatever it is you fancy or imagine is sure to be available. Top quality products of some of the most popular name brands as well as locally produced goods are in Tokyo, making it a favorite shopping destination for many travelers. Spend a day walking and exploring the streets of the shopping district. Take time to take in the scene from the sidewalk and you might just find a traditional tea house where you can duck into to experience a little taste of one of their many traditions. Walk lightly and take in sights, sounds and smells that will feed your senses. Follow your nose and feed your tummy at some of the finest restaurant the city metropolis has to offer. Sample the seasonal fare that is specific to the period of the year. Tokyo, would obviously have some of the best sushi bars that serve up not only your favorite rice rolls, you can also try some of the more local fare not available in your local Japanese restaurant.

And with a vibrant, lively nightlife, you can be sure that there will always be something's new and interesting to discover. You will find Tokyo evenings to be magical and electric all at once and is well known for its legendary nightlife. Take a stroll around and be delighted with the little "discoveries" you will find along the way.

There will never be a shortage of things to do with the city's countless boutiques, restaurants, arcades, waterholes, dance halls, and cubs. Have a drink or two at some of the best bars around the city or duck into one of the traditional Japanese bars that little thoroughfares and you might just discover. There are hundreds of hotels and boutique hotels that will fit your budget that will allow you a place to rest your head and recharge for another go at the city.

Let us give you an advance tour of Tokyo to help prepare your itinerary when your hit the Land of the Rising Sun!

Table of Contents

An Introduction to Tokyo 1

   Tokyo in Focus..3

   A Brief History of Tokyo 6

Chapter One: Tokyo's Culture and People............................11

   Tokyo in Focus..12

   Languages in Tokyo, Japan..17

   The Japanese People...20

Chapter Two: Travel Essentials..23

   Japan Visa and Passport Requirements 25

   Seasons in Tokyo 27

Chapter Three: Getting In and Around...................................31

Tokyo...31

   Transportation 35

Chapter Four: Budget-Friendly Hotels and Accommodations

in Tokyo 39

   Richmond Hotel Asakusa – Best location 46

   The Andon Ryokan 48

Hotel Fukudaya 50

Tokyo Green Hotel Korakuen 52

Chiyoda Inn... 54

Coco Grand Kitasenju.. 57

Chapter Five: Dining in the City Metropolis........... 59

Ginza Kyubey 61

Kanda 63

Ginza Kojyu.. 65

Ivy Place.. 71

Sukiyabashi Jiro 72

Higashiyama 74

Takazawa... 76

Sushi Saito 78

Some Tips When Dining in Japan 80

Chapter Six: Shopping in Tokyo 83

Shibuya Shopping District 85

Ginza 88

Kōenji... 91

Asakusa...94

Akihabara 99

Shinjuku 102

Chapter Seven: Tourist Spots in Tokyo...............105

Tokyo Disneyland 106

Tokyo Sea Life Park...108

The Imperial Palace...110

Tokyo National Museum 112

Tokyo National Museum of Emerging Science and

Innovation...114

Tokyo Metropolitan Government Building.....................116

Shinjuku Gyoen National Garden.......................118

Tokyo Tower 119

Ghilbi Museum 121

Tsukiji Market 123

Chapter Eight: Tokyo Shrines and Temples.........125

Meiji-Jingu Shrine...127

Tennoji Temple 129

Yasukuni Shrine..130

Koganji Temple..132

Akagi Shrine..133

Nezu Shrine...134

Yushima Seido Temple.......................................136

Narita-san Fukagawa Fudo-Do Temple...............138

Yushima Tenjin Shrine.......................................140

Chapter Nine: Nightlife in Tokyo 143

Bar High Five 146

AgeHa 149

Mandarin Bar 151

Ben Fiddich...153

Meishu Center Tokyo-Sake Tasting Bar...............156

Gaspanic..159

Chapter Ten:..161

Last Minute Traveller Tips.................................161

Important Guidelines...163

Mingle and Mix...164

Heads Up! 165

Worth the Visit! 167

PHOTO REFERENCES 173

REFERENCES 185

An Introduction to Tokyo

You can try looking for a place similar to it the world over, but you will not find anything quite like Tokyo. Here is where harmony and symmetry blend the old and traditional with the mega retail centers, ambitious skyscrapers and futuristic technology seamlessly. The densely inhabited city that sits on earthquake prone land has tested the resilience of the city metropolis time and again. Admirably, despite challenges, the unwavering can-do spirit of Tokyo and its locals shine and inspire the rest of the world.

The impressive landscape of the city metropolis glimmering against the night sky is a sight straight out of the imaginings of forward thinking, future-centric designers and builders.

Tucked away in the shadow of mega structures and towering skyscrapers, the quaint charm of the old world Nippon is alive, well and evident. Little reminders of the humble beginnings of Tokyo are found on the kabuki stages, and sumo tournaments. It is experienced in anachronistic wooden shanties that serve either as a bar or a tea room, where the meditative tradition of tea preparation is deliberate and thoughtfully performed to this day. It is seen in the manner of everyday life and magnified by the almost tribal-like fervor of festivals observed by the residents of the city metropolis.

Tokyo in Focus

Made up of 23 municipalities, which collectively make up the heart of the metropolitan prefecture that is uniquely Tokyo, it possesses a distinction which is unlike any of the major cities of the world. The municipality's spread out over the land and is clustered in this region of Japan originally known as Edo. When the Emperor Meiji transferred his seat of emperorship from Kyoto to Edo in 1868, the metropolis was soon after renamed Tokyo. Its status was only fairly recently declared in 1943, after the merger of the Tokyo prefecture and the city of Tokyo transformed the region and grew to be one of the largest metropolis we presently know. The metropolitan government of Tokyo manages the 23 Special Wards of Tokyo, governing each ward as a separate city. Aside from the 23 special wards the Tokyo metropolitan government oversees, it also administers to two island chains of the region and 39 other municipalities in the west end of the Tokyo prefecture.

All these tiny city clusters were collectively pooled together to make up what is now the vibrant and ever burgeoning Tokyo Metropolis. To illustrate and understand the method of governance better, these 23 special wards of Tokyo can be likened to the boroughs of New York City or the London boroughs, and operates much in a similar manner. The city of Tokyo is officially governed as a metropolitan prefecture which has distinction, and greatly differs, from the methods of administration and mechanics of operations of a city. Tokyo has, with admirable grace, continues to evolve, combining a plethora of elements and ingredients which make up a city metropolis that enviable as it is inspiring. It stands out as a shining example of how the mix of winning ingredients of passion, imagination, ambition, respect toward self and others, reverence in use of resources, and decided commitment to progress.

Tokyo was the seat of influence for the Meiji Emperor during his era, and so it remains true today with the reigning monarch, Emperor Akihito. Here in the city of Tokyo, is where the governance of Nippon sits. It is one of the 47 prefectures in Japan and is the most populous area in the whole world, with a total headcount of a whopping 13 million inhabitants. It is situated   in the region of Kanto - on the southeastern part of the island of Honshu. Tokyo has consistently been recognized as an economic power seat, sitting on top rank in the Global Economic Power Index. The Globalization and World Cities Research Network, in 2008, listed Tokyo as an alpha world city, playing a major role in the global economic system. Studies and observation have proven that the backbone of a good economy is the provision of roads which allow for transport accessible because allows for convenient access to vital point to point destinations.

A Brief History of Tokyo

Once upon a long time ago, between a long span of period from 1185 to 1868, the land of the Rising Sun and all its inhabitants were headed by the military dictatorship of the shogun and the shogunate. These brave, military men, who were appointed by the Emperor ruled the land of cherry blossoms and were respected, if not feared, shoguns - the short form for Sei-i Taishōgun. The Sei-i Taishōgun, who were appointed by the Emperor to position, ruled the land and its territories with absolute power. Their rule, or bakufu, employed military means to defend their land and keep the peace from rivals and opposition military government .The title of shogun, or the Commander In Chief of the Expeditionary Force Against Barbarians, was bestowed upon military commanders during the Heian period. During this period they launched military campaigns on those who resisted the governance of the imperial court in Kyoto. The imperial court had little authority over the shoguns, since the office of the shogun ruled much like a viceroy, exercising their authority over the people of the land on behalf of the monarchy. In truth, shoguns wielded more power. Even the reigning Emperor of those bygone times took directives from the office of the shogun until the end of feudalism.

The bustling, and equally tranquil city of Tokyo was once called Edo, which means "estuary" because of its close proximity to the delta. Edo became the high perch of power ruled by the Tokugawa shogunate. The bakufu of Tokugawa lorded over Japan from 1603 to 1868 and it richly burgeoned under the leadership, becoming a contender as one of the largest cities in the world. The Edo-period was immersed in a culture of urban living. The city sought the pleasures of life and lived the ukiyo culture.

The culture of the Floating World first came about in the licensed red-light district in Yoshiwara. The district was teeming with kabuki theatres, tea houses, and bordellos which the prominent middle class frequented. The ukiyo way of life found its way in the nearby cities of Kyoto and Osaka.

Edo, in effect, became the center of power due to the Tokugawa bakufu headquarters which was housed in the growing coastal town. However, for all intents and purposes, the proper capital of Japan then was still in Kyoto. Sure enough, Edo grew and prospered from the small, coastal, fishing village it started out as into a large, bustling metropolis. Before Edo officially became Tokyo, the city metropolis experienced repeated devastation caused by accidental fires, earthquakes and armed conflict.

The city of Edo was renamed Tokyo in 1868, when the rulership of the shogunate ended. Shortly after, the emperor took up his imperial residence in the newly christened city of Tokyo, sealing its position as the true capital of Nippon.

The long rich history of Tokyo is a fascinating one indeed and it continues to write its history today.

Marrying the elements of a prefecture and the busy activities of a city, Tokyo has surely marked its position on the map as a unique combination of a metropolitan prefecture.

Chapter One: Tokyo's Culture and People

Every country has their own special characteristics and unique qualities that make them distinct and one of a kind and Japan is no different. Although Japanese people are pretty polite and will not call you out on something they may find offensive, Japanese people will surely be impressed with the homework you've done. Apart from the customs that are uniquely Japanese, there are things about the culture that you would find interesting as well as utilitarian for your quick visit there.

In addition to these, we are also throwing in, what some would consider to be, odd practices that are acceptable (or otherwise) in Japan.

Tokyo in Focus

When in Tokyo, to avoid faux pas and risk offending any of the locals we came up with a short list of some of the more interesting bits about Japanese customs and culture that would really come handy before heading down to the Land of the Rising Sun.

One of the things that are foremost in this mention is respect. Respect, and the show of it, is very important in the Japanese culture. The Japanese people are very big on respect for each other and doing your bit to find out more about the country, the culture and the people gives you a better advantage of mingling with the locals and enjoying the sights and sounds of the perpetually on the move city of Tokyo. Upon introductions, the exchange of wares or money, the act of saying farewell and so on are just of the many instances you will find locals greeting and ending the meet with a bow. This culture of respect is apparent in everyday life and is a refreshing trait that is not seen in most countries of the world.

Upon your arrival on Japanese shores, you will notice the mindfulness people pay to others. Japanese culture inculcates mindfulness of others,

- On slurping your food. I am willing to bet the money in my pocket that this is not something that would be done where you are from and anyone at a dinner table who does may get reprimanded by mother. Not so in Japan. In fact, if you are going to try that ramen house down the corner, you may hear a lot of slurping going on, and that is perfectly normal. In fact it is expected. For one noisily slurping noodles into your mouth cools the noodles as they go in your pie-hole and the slurpy noises you make is a compliment to the chef to signal that you find this particular bowl prepared for you to be delicious.

- Unlike most countries in the world where people are not allowed to drink on the streets and would most likely get fined or incarcerated for it, this just isn't so in Japan. The country is lax about consuming alcohol in public and has no open container laws. Although you won't usually see locals drinking on a street corner from a bottle, it is not unusual to see groups of people or lone individuals, hanging out at the park, having a picnic and throwing back a couple of pints of beer.

- Since Japanese people work, not only long hours, but diligently as well, it is not uncommon for office workers to either stay long after work hours to put in overtime work or to knock back a few after quitting time as a way to unwind, or show team spirit. People passed out near subway stations are not that unusual to see in the busy business districts of Tokyo. The very least these people get is quietly laughed at by passersby, but no one has gotten mugged or stolen from. It is the intrinsic trust system that operates amongst the locals of Japan that one would not have to worry about their valuables being taken from them whilst sleeping it off. Traveling alone and worried about leaving your bags at your table but afraid of losing if you left them? Worry not. People in Tokyo don't even think twice about leaving their bags, phones, gadgets, bicycles and motorcycles unattended and it would be right where you left it when you get back.

- Smoking is still allowed in most places in Japan. Japan is one of the few countries who have not imposed any smoking laws and lighting up in bars, pubs and restaurants are not unusual. If you are a smoker this could be good news. If you aren't then this would be good to know before you start loudly objecting and get surprised by the lack of concern. However, there are considerations for those who do not smoke because there are actual designated areas for smokers. You have to remember that Tokyo's original culture, the mindset of the city when it was first founded, was one where people were able to

- There are quite a few things that are usual in Japan that people would not be able to get away with in other countries. Apart from smoking and public consumption of alcohol, pornographic material is easily obtainable through your local bookstore or magazine stand. Adult-themed manga is not uncommon reading material amongst people in the big cities. This is not unusual in Japan and if you knew to look, even some of the more mundane, regular magazine on a rack will probably have a page or two of adult-themed comics or literature. A good thing to keep in mind is that when buying adult manga books at bookstores, one can have their books covered.

Languages in Tokyo, Japan

The people of Japan speak a variety of dialects; many of these are indigenous to regions of the country and have been declared endangered languages by the UNESCO. Many of these endangered languages within Japan are not mutually intelligible with each other or Japanese. The spoken language in Japan is Japanese and is divided to many dialects including that spoken in Tokyo.

In other parts of Japan, aside from Japanese, languages like Ryukyuan which is spoken in parts of Kagoshima as well as Okinawa. The indigenous people of the island of Ainu in Hokkaido speak the Ainu language (aside from the more common Japanese).

The main language spoken in Tokyo is the Tokyo dialect and is what is widely known as the Japanese language throughout the world. You'll be pleased to know that you will not necessarily have to learn these dialects of Japan to get by. In Tokyo, the most common Japanese dialect is Nihongo (Japanese). It will not be unusual to hear people say Nippongo, too, but this is more nationalistic as opposed to the more neutral Nihongo. The characters you will see on street and indoor signages will be written in kanji characters.

Tokyo has been host to a hodgepodge of cultures. Because of economic booms and business expansions, Tokyo has been the home of many international companies equating to migrations of people from all over the world. That being said, Tokyo is still largely populated by locals from the city metropolis and citizens of Japan from other regions of the country. You will find that English is widely understood and spoken, albeit a little sheepishly, most especially in the districts where tourists can be found the most. The language of Japan, once said to be the most confusing, befuddling language to strangers of the country, can indeed be daunting more the untrained, so the two-part bit of information will bring you good news.

First is that, almost all signs (that concern you as a tourist) all over the city metropolis caters to Japanese and English speakers. That means most signs for the WC, entrance; exit, etc. will not only be in Japanese, it will be in English as well. If lost and in doubt, you should be able to tell where you are, at the very least. Although most travel agents in the US and Japan encourage guided tours throughout Tokyo, you will be surprised and pleased to discover that with a little bit of research you can actually get by without sweating the small stuff too much.

Of course, given the limited amount of time you are allowed in the country, understanding what to expect is always a good place to start. After all you don't want to be the one creating numerous mistakes. Second is that, the people of Tokyo are some of the most helpful people on the planet. They would gladly give you a hand if you were lost. This now brings us to our next section - the people of Tokyo.

The Japanese People

The Japanese is a truly a culture that is really their marked own. They are a very perceptive sort of people who are naturally in tune with other people around them. They are mindful of each other's spaces and respect each other's time. Some of the best examples of the mindfulness people of Tokyo practice can be on escalators, trains and public places.

Locals do not talk loudly on their phones, they are not taken to shoving people aside to get a better space in a crowded train, and they do not talk loudly in public places and are truly helpful. It would do you well to memorize a few polite phrases in Japanese. The locals of the city metropolis will be impressed and tickled pink to hear a foreigner take time to learn a little of their language.

Chapter Two: Travel Essentials

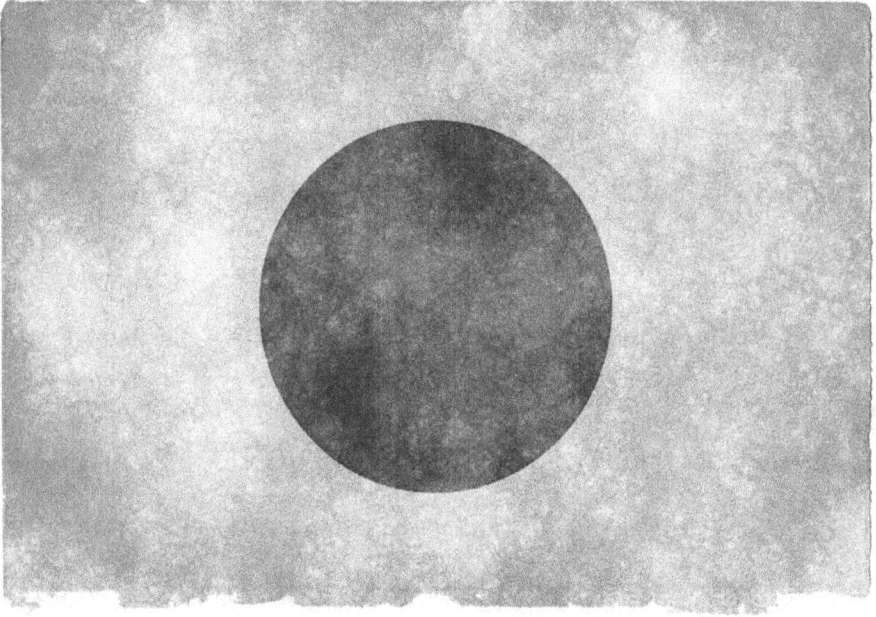

Smart travellers make it a point to prepare for their holidays long before the actual trip and this is just as it should be if you want to make the most out of your vacation holiday. There are a few important details to tick off your checklist to ensure a speedy, uncomplicated transit and entry to any country you desire. Save for some countries with special ties and agreements with Japan, most citizens of the countries of the world will need to apply for a Japanese visa if they wish to travel to the Land of Cherry Blossoms, and all will need a passport at the very least.

And every one will need to present a valid airline ticket to the country. In some cases, a traveller with more than one leg of trip will need to present their connecting tickets at the airport immigration of the countries of their destination and departure.

Apart from the travel documents required of you when traveling out of your home country, it is also equally important to pack smartly for your trip out the land of the rising sun. The stuff you pack and bring with you on the trip will depend not only on the month of the year, but also the sort of activities you plan on doing there. Since Tokyo experiences four seasons of the year, it would serve you best to know about when these events of the season take place.

Japan Visa and Passport Requirements

Before you buy those costly tickets and make those lavish hotel reservations, make sure you have the most important things covered and available first! Unless you've discovered the secret of teleportation, any trip outside of your home country would most certainly require you to present your travel passport. Having your passport always ready and available allows you the advantage of planning trips with one thing less to worry about. Make sure that your passport is valid and that it will be valid upon your return to your home country.

Citizens of the United States are not given permission to work in Japan using their 90-day visa-free entry to the land of the Rising Sun. Generally, a 90-day visa-free entry status cannot be upgraded or changed to another status without the act of leaving the country and re-entering again, with the proper visa status. This visa status could be for work, study or spousal visa.

Any United States citizen who intends to visit Japan will need to make sure that their passport is valid for the duration of the visit and is accompanied by a corresponding and valid visa, should there be trip take longer than the 90-day visa free stay. Be mindful that your passports are valid for the whole duration of the stay because there are no consulate services at the airport. Although some airline individuals do notice, it is not the airline's responsibility to check the validity of your travel documents.

Not having the proper travel documents i.e. passport, visa, valid return ticket runs you the risk of getting whisked onto the airplane only to be sent back to your home country, at your expense, because of an expired passport. If you are visiting then transiting through Japan, it will be up to you to ensure that all your travelling papers are in order, up to date and valid for all ports of entry and exit.

Seasons in Tokyo

When you have all these necessary travel papers in order (your passport and visa to Japan) you can start looking into getting tickets. You will want to determine which time of the year you intend to visit Tokyo, to determine the sort of clothes you need to carry with you, and what sort of weather waits for you upon your arrival. The seasons in Japan are pretty distinct and this is good to know because you want to be able to pack for the right season you will be going there.

To make the most out of your Japan trip, the best time to enjoy the mild climate would be during springtime from March to May. This happens when the famous cherry blossoms of Japan are on full display and the days are temperate enough to tour the main districts and side thoroughfares. These months are comfortably warmer without being uncomfortably hot. You will want to make sure to pack a sweater for the evenings when it can get a little chilly.

The end of April and the beginning of May has notably more tourists of the international and local kind, with the Golden Week of Japan in full swing. The Golden Week, as it is called, is the period towards the last week of April to the first week of May, when concentrations of national holidays are observed. It may well be the busiest time of the year in relation to the city metropolis receiving visitors. This is probably best avoided especially if you want to experience a more personal, more personalized visit to the city.

To allow for an unimpeded journey in discovery of the city metropolis and the surrounding prefectures of Tokyo, pack a small umbrella for each person on the trip. A light, rainproof jacket is also advisable for any unexpected showers you may get caught under.

The summer months are experienced between June to August and this can be a pretty challenging weather if you are not used to the heat. Even those used to experiencing this sort of heat try to stay out of the oppressive humidity when they can, locals either go off to places where the weather is cooler or look for places where they can enjoy beach fronts. It is still pretty usual for Tokyo to experience chance showers, so be ready and prepared for any sudden weather changes. Make sure that you pack clothes that are comfortable, and light. Make sure that you do not carry anything too heavy that will not dry up easily in case of a downpour.

September is not the best time to move around in Tokyo since this is usually the time of year when the weather can be more unpredictable and the city is more prone to typhoons. It would probably be wisest to hold off your traipse around the richly historical, and electrically charged city metropolis. You will have a better bet of enjoying the off-beat vibe of Tokyo around October when humidity is lower compared to the summer months but still find it comfortably snug as long as you bundle up well. Winter in Tokyo is crisp, and clear. The city metropolis hardly, if it ever does, get snow so if you were looking for an alternative venue for a White Christmas you will probably have better chances going further up north to the island of Hokkaido, considered as the Alps of Japan.

Chapter Three: Getting In and Around Tokyo

Tokyo has one of the most advanced transportation systems, it is no wonder that the metropolis has consistently placed first with TripAdvisor in the category of the city that provides the "best in overall travel experience". You will find that people from Tokyo, are a willingly, open and helpful bunch of people who would be happy to point out the way to your destination. The trick is to speak clearly and avoid jargon and usual phrases in English that may confound your friendly local.

Unless you have a personal English speaking guide, you will want to remember that most temple and national shrine tours are only carried out in Japanese. If you happen to find yourself outside of Tokyo, for one reason or another, and you are in need of assistance in English, you may want to jot down the number for the toll-free Travel Phone Information - 106. If you need help to get to a phone, simply write the number down on a piece of paper and ask for a phone as you present the piece of paper with the number. When in Tokyo, the number for the Travel Phone Service is 502-1461. The Travel Phone Service is manned between the hours of 9am to 5pm daily. Once connected, speak slowly and clearly to the person on the other line and say "T.I.C." which is short for Tourist Information Center. Once you are connected to the TIC, tell them of your location and ask your question. The T.I.C. is part of the Japan National Tourist Organization.

Another option you may also check out, is the unofficial information desk located at the entrances of most major department stores of the city metropolis, where there always seem to be an English-speaking person present and on duty. They will be happy to help you with most things, as long as they know where to point you, but they will largely be concerned about information inside the complex. One bit of information you may want to keep in mind is that, it is easier to encash the traveller's cheques at the information desk of a major retail complex than it is at a bank, as long as you have your passport with you.

Sign language, if employed clearly enough, can certainly be an acceptable form of communication. For all intents and purposes, memorizing a few lines in Nihongo can help you go a long way.

- dozo (DOH-zo) - Please, after you

- sumimasen (soo-MEE-mah-sehn) - Pardon me

- domo arigato (DOH-moh-ah-REE-gah-toh) - Thank you

- do itashi mashite (doh-ee TAH-shee-mahsh-teh) - You're welcome

- hajime mahite (hah-JEE-meh-mahsh-teh) How do you do?

- ohayo gozaimasu (oh-HAH-yoh goh-ZAH-ee-mahs)

- kon nichi wa (KOHN-nee-chee-wah) Good afternoon

- komban wa (KOHN-bahn-wah) - Good evening

- hai (HAH-eh) - Yes

- iie (ee-EH) - No

Transportation

The two major airports in Tokyo is the Narita Airport, located 60 km outside of the centre of the city metropolis, which has the majority of international flights coming through its airspace, and a small number of domestic flights as well and the Haneda Airport with a smaller number of international flights, and mainly relegated to handling the majority of domestic flights coming into to Tokyo. Most of the shinkansen lines, or the fast speed trains, lead up to Tokyo, so if you were looking to venture outside of the city metropolis for a bit, it might serve you best to make these arrangements before the beginning of your trip to Tokyo, in order to familiarize yourself with your chosen route and to secure your train tickets in advance.

There are about a dozen various transportation operators that operate within the city that is covered with a vast network of subway and train lines and bus routes. Look out for the JR East train and subway lines because this is probably the most conveniently efficient way of getting around the center of Tokyo. The loop line of the prominent JR Yamanote Line is one that connects Tokyo to multiple city centres. The Yamanote Line is one that circles and connects all the major city centres of Tokyo.

Running parallel on the eastern half of the Yamanote Line Loop is Keihin-Tohoku Line, serving central Tokyo and the nearby prefectures of Kanagawa and Saitama City on the north and Yokohama and Kawasaki in the South. The Chuo/Sobu Line is a local line which runs across the Yamanote Loop. The Rapid Chuo Line is a faster service train that also runs across the Yamanote Loop and connects with the Shinjuku Station as well as the Tokyo Station.

The Saikyo Line traverses parallel to the Yamanote Line on the western portion of the loop. Some trains continue to operate along the Rinkai Line from the Osaki Station toward the direction of Odaiba. And then you have the Tokaido Shinkansen train which stops at the Tokyo and Shinagawa stations with the bullet trains of the north stopping at Ueno and Tokyo stations.

Most shinkansen in Japan has two sorts of seats offered to the riding public and these seat classes are found in separate cars. Ordinary seats are available in all shinkansen trains; however there are variations in terms of the foot space across the various trains on the line. In spite of the differences in foot space and seats, the ordinary seats of the shinkansen are actually quite comfortable and have adequate to generous leg room. The green car is what can be compared to a business class flight on an airplane. The green coach train seats are a lot wider and have a lot more leg room, tending to be less crowded than the ordinary cars.

The Gran Class is now available on the newer sets of trains and can be compared to first class seats on an airplane. The Gran Class has 2 spacious side by side seats. Make sure that you make prior reservations for seats in the reserved car. Be prepared to pay for the seat reservation which costs a few hundred yen. On the other hand, if you are holding a Japan Rail Pass, you can make reservations with no additional cost to you.

Chapter Four: Budget-Friendly Hotels and Accommodations in Tokyo

It is no wonder people visit Tokyo, Japan. Tokyo is such a vibrant city with a very rich culture and a long history. Smart and frugal travelers to the city look for decent yet affordable accommodations so that they can spend their travel budget on other things such as food, tourist attractions and keepsakes. Are you one of them? If you are then you will be truly pleased to know that there are a number of budget-friendly hotels in Tokyo that will fit your budget and afford you the comforts of a respite away from home. Despite its reputation of being one of the most expensive cities in the world, Tokyo has made it a point to make the majesty and beauty of the city accessible to the many travelers of the world who are just itching to discover the beauty of the Land of the Rising Sun.

As you plan on booking a budget-friendly hotel to stay in, keep in mind that compared to Western hotels, the rooms are not as spacious but it is not to say that you will be housed in a crate! Some of the most comfortable stays are the list of accommodations we have compiled for you and you will surely find one that not only fits your budget but will give you a memorable stay as well.

Do remember that upon checking in you will be required to present your passport for purposes of identification and registration. There are hotels that showcase Japanese traditions and conveniences such as floor mats instead of the usual beds, public spas, massage chairs and tea service and then there are those that are more the conventional hotel rooms with the usual amenities.

Here is our list of top 10 best budget hotels in Tokyo to help you plan your accommodations:

Sakura Hotel Hatagaya

The Sakura Hotel Hatagaya is tagged as one of the best budget hotels in Tokyo. And here are some reasons why it is so. First of all, it is conveniently located in the vibrantly exciting district of Shibuya, where there is great shopping to be had and a major strolling district where you can find all sorts and all kinds of interesting shops, restaurants and cafes. It is also in a fairly quiet residential area. This budget-friendly, yet super cozy hotel boasts of a lustrous interior design and extravagant amenities. At an affordable price, you can enjoy the following features that go with your room like a private bath, cooling air conditioner, television and free Wi-Fi.

Hotel Niwa Tokyo

Another hotel that is labelled as one of the best accommodations in the city is the Hotel Niwa Tokyo. Guests of the city metropolis will have a really enjoyable stay owing to the following features of this 38-room hotel that will be welcome warmth at the end of a long day about the city. The Hotel Niwa has a gym you can duck into for a quick workout during your vacation. I also have a quaint outdoor courtyard that invites the soul and body to relax. Make sure that you mention whether you prefer a smoking or non-smoking room when making your reservations.

Guests can choose from two dining options to enjoy sumptuous meals anytime of the day with the French restaurant, Lieu, that serves up fine French cuisine using seasonal ingredients and the Japanese restaurant, Yukuri, which boasts of some of the most loved dishes of the country, you can be sure your meals are covered, whether breakfast, lunch or dinner. The rooms are modern in design, soundproof, air-conditioned. Rooms are furnished with a mini-ref which you can use to stock up on drinks and snacks. The hotel offers free internet access. The streamlined, minimal and modern interior decor makes for a relaxing nap and a good night's sleep.

Shiba Park Hotel

It can be difficult to find an affordable hotel that is big enough for everyone in the brood when you are travelling with your family. This is why the following advantages make the Shiba Park Hotel one of the best hotels for travelling families.

With clean, spacious rooms that have the necessary amenities of modern living the Shiba Park Hotel promises to be the welcoming refuge for your weary feet and body after a long day of getting about town. When most other hotels in the city have small rooms with no option of adjoining rooms, the Shiba Park Hotel offers their guests room options to choose from. With their triple, quad or connecting rooms, no family is too big for this hotel.

The Shiba Park Hotel offers free accommodations for children below seven years old to share an existing bed. Extra costs are optional furniture you can ask about. The upgraded Shiba Park Hotel is very near the Daimon and Onarimon subway making it easy for families to get around with the kids in tow. The recently refurbished hotel has two restaurants where guests can enjoy their meals. The Japanese restaurant offers up some of the best and most favorite dishes served in the country. It also houses a Chinese restaurant which serves up some of the best dishes. For a nightcap after a long day walking and exploring the magnificent city of Tokyo duck into the Grill, a lounge/bar where you can have a nightcap or two and enjoy an animated chat with your companions..

Richmond Hotel Asakusa – Best location

The budget hotel that can be described as the best location to stay in when in Tokyo is the Richmond Hotel Asakusa because guests of this hotel can practically explore all of Tokyo from this basecamp. With various transportation options nearby such as the Toei Asakusa Line, Tobu Skytree Line and Tsukuba Express Line, guests of the Richmond is only a mere-minutes away from the thick of the action. The world-renowned Sensoji Temple is just a stone's throw away and within walking distance. Guests of the Richmond get an amazing view of the city from the higher level rooms if booked in advance.

The upper level suites afford a great vantage point of the city minus the noise of the traffic below. There are 270 ultra-modern rooms that are decorated tastefully and furnished essentially for comfort. Each room has air conditioning with bath and toilet supplied with the necessary bath essentials. Guests also enjoy access to free, stable internet connection. There is also a business center on site for anything you might need to fulfill for work. Accommodations come with a hearty buffet breakfast served in a dining area with a view.

The Andon Ryokan

If you are a smaller party of two and want to take advantage of making the best of the city metropolis, but want comfy, but affordable accommodations, then the Andon Ryokan may just be the hotel for you. Book a 75-square feet room at the Andon Ryokan located at 2 Chome-34-10 Nihonzutsumi, Taitō, Tokyo, and experience the simplicity of Tokyo living, with the basic modern amenities of today, like Internet, TV, etc. Not only will you save a pretty penny, you will also be able to enjoy the benefits of the minimal design and simplistic furnishings using authentic and traditional Japanese antique decor and furnishings.

Mingling with other travelers is encouraged during breakfast. Make a few friends during a customary Japanese tea ceremony. The Andon Ryokan offers the escape from the world below with a rooftop terrace where guests can enjoy a view of the city and have picnics. Guests also have the option reserve and use a Jacuzzi for free, and are encouraged to book this when they book their accommodation. Adding to the charm and beauty of the experience, the hotel staff of the Andon Ryokan is very friendly and accommodating.

Hotel Fukudaya

Book your stay at the Hotel Fukudaya and get a taste of traditional Japanese accommodations that is easy on the wallet and won't break the bank. Located conveniently on 4 Chome-5-9 Aobadai, Meguro, Tokyo 153-004, the Hotel Fukudaya boasts of the understated basic comforts of a traditional Japanese home whilst making you feel like the guest you are. Experience the old-world luxury of an authentic ryokan which offer traditional Japanese beddings in intimate settings.

The Hotel Fukudaya is a compact but very comfortable and very clean hotel that has a total of 17 rooms. Thirteen of the seventeen rooms here have interiors in minimalist fashion which is furnished with the basic futon beddings set on traditional tatami mats completed by buckwheat-filled pillows. If you would rather have the more conventional beds much like the ones you have at home, you may inquire about and book one of the four western-styled rooms. The hotel is highly accessible, being 15 minutes away from the Shibuya Metro Station.

Tokyo Green Hotel Korakuen

Another hotel within the city metropolis and one which is a stone's throw away as it is easily accessible from the Tokyo Station and Shinjuku Station is the Tokyo Green Hotel Korakuen. Located on 1-1-3, Koraku, Bunkyo-ku,Tokyo, 112-0004, this hotel is literally right where journeys start and destinations, arrived. If you intend on or compelled to concentrating you're wandering in the center of the city, or if you have business in the central district of Tokyo, this hotel may be the best one for you.

The location of the hotel is perfect for visitors who want to be in the heart of the city and the action. Choose from any of their spacious and elegantly simple rooms that are utterly comfortable and spotless. Guests of the Tokyo Green Hotel Korakuen enjoys free internet access in these modestly, and comfortably furnished rooms. And because of the hotel's close proximity to different shops, bars and fine-dining restaurants in the city getting around on foot will be a pleasure as it will be an experience!

Chiyoda Inn

If you are a visitor who prefers a less busy area, check into the friendly Chiyoda Inn and enjoy at affordable rates which allow you to spend your money on gathering and collecting good memories of Tokyo, Get the feel of "home away from home." The Chiyoda Inn offers small and cozy rooms that are fit for one to two guests and is furnished sparsely. The minimal décor allows for one to single beds to a room, a desk and shared bathrooms.

Prefer to have a washroom, toilet n your own room? Then ask about the traditional Japanese rooms

Sakura Hotel Jimbocho

If you want the best access to various tourist attractions, the Sakura Hotel Jimbocho on 5 Chome-33-9 Minami Senju, Arakawa, Tokyo 116-0003 is a hotel you might want to consider. Being in such close proximity to the more popular shopping places and must-see spots in Tokyo, the Sakura promises one to be an arm's length away from everything that's happening in the city metropolis.

If you saved up for other memories to invest on and don't want to spend too much on accommodations, there is no better place to stay than where the hub of the action is and the Sakura Hotel Jimbocho is just where it's at. With the much-visited Tokyo Station, Nippon Budokan, Tokyo Dome and the Imperial Palace, which may have been what well beckoned you over, and restaurants and shops all within walking distance from the hotel, how can you go wrong? The rooms at the Sakura Hotel Jimbocho are simple yet cozy; with all the basic amenities and a little extra to make sure you have a comfortable stay. This hotel is great for young backpackers and families on vacation.

Coco Grand Kitasenju

Looking for a budget hotel that offers a touch of pampering? Book your stay at the Coco Grand Kitasenju. Guests of the hotel can get an amazing view of the city from any of the 100 rooms of the hotel. Standard rooms come with pajamas and massage chairs as well as complimentary Wi - Fi. Guests of the Coco Grand Kita Senju will enjoy both Japanese and Western cuisine for their free breakfast buffet, as the kitchen serves up scrumptious meals to get you through the morning of exploration and visitations.

For the sweet tooth, the hotel also boasts of a dessert shop and Japanese bakery where local pastries that are all time favorites can be purchased and enjoyed. The hotel offers the use of a public bath (spa) on the hotel's second floor, for me. And Women also have the opportunity to enjoy the hot rocks and dry sauna that the hotel boasts.

When travelling to a new country, or just travelling for that matter, securing a place to stay is important in order for you to be able to focus and enjoy your trip. If you know where to look, hotels in Tokyo are not as expensive as you would think and you won't have to stay in capsule hotels unless of course that is the experience you want. Even for 3 or 3.5-star hotels, you can expect great service and value for your money. Keep in mind though, when you book during Saturdays or peak seasons, you may have to pay an additional 30% on regular rates because of the surge in demand. Additionally, you may have to book at least 3 months in advance if you plan on going during super peak seasons of the autumn foliage and cherry blossoms.

Chapter Five: Dining in the City Metropolis

Tokyo boasts of being called home to some of the most lauded and applauded Michelin-starred restaurants in the world. Expect to have some of the best dining experiences in the city that serves up some of the most diverse cuisines and restaurants. When people think of Tokyo, they are immediately reminded of sushi. However, Tokyo is more than just sushi, although there are awesome sushi bars to visit and try out, visitors and foodies alike will get enjoy a wide array of authentic Japanese cuisine such as tonkatsu, okonomiyaki and unagi eel.

You don't have to be intimidated by all the Michelin starred restaurants as you will also gleefully discover little tucked-away pub grubs, cafés and hole-in-the-wall bars all over the city. Overall, Tokyo is a nirvana for travel and food lovers, waiting to be discovered and found out. Don't be surprised to make a new friend out of the many experiences you will have during these meals at common restaurants of the city. This chapter will cover 10 of the best restaurants that serve up some of the best in Japanese cuisine and world-class dishes that will make your memories of Tokyo even sweeter.

Ginza Kyubey

It must be a given. When in Tokyo scouting out and zeroing in on sushi has to be on top of the list. The flagship restaurant of the Kyubey family is a very popular restaurant in the city that offers so much. Kyubey is considered the sushi empire with the main location housed in a five-story high building, with an annex across the street and is constantly with patrons waiting to get their specialized sushi rolls in an efficiently, amusing manner.

As if that were not testament enough to the sushi empire's popularity, there are four more other branches of the Ginza Kyubey at different luxury hotels.

Kimono-clad ushers welcome guests to this intimate 4-storey eating place, making the experience feel special and ritualistic. Guests have the option to dine in private counter spaces that have low tables and tatami mats. Enjoy the best sushi in Tokyo at a very convivial atmosphere and allow the reality of you being a world away from home, as you enjoy the novelty of the moment. While the sushi is quite pricey compared to other restaurants, you can consider it a bargain because of its quality of freshness and care put into constructing your food. You won't have a hard time making reservations and walk-ins are also welcome.

To get there, just take the Shimbashi Station in order to get to the restaurant, which is located on 8 Chome-7-6 Ginza, Chūō, Tokyo 104-0061. The set price for a 5-dish dinner or lunch is around 17,700 yen. Reservations are recommended and you can pay by cash or credit card.

Kanda

You will be surprised to know that this 8-seater restaurant found on an anonymous building at one of the backstreets of Tokyo is rated 3 Michelin stars. Book a table at least a couple of months ahead so you can be sure to experience popular Japanese contemporary cuisine by Chef Hiroyuki Kanda. Chefs will prepare dishes at the counter while you watch. You will enjoy the demonstration of their knife skills as they pay careful detail to the presentation of dishes.

While there is no menu, expect to savor seasonal dishes that appear in a string along the wooden counter. There is also sake and a good wine selection. The draft beer is divine and goes well with the fare prepared and served up before you. The restaurant is at Motoazabu, Minato-ku and you can take the Roppongi Station to get there. Reservations are required and dinner set menu prices start at 25,000 yen for 9- or 10-courses.

Ginza Kojyu

If you want to experience the traditional multi-course Japanese dinner (referred to as kaiseki dining), then you should drop by Ginza Kojyu. Prepare yourself to be fully satisfied and get a memorable introduction to the Japanese cuisine. The cozy interior of the place will remind you of well-loved homestyle cooking. Watch your dishes being skillfully prepared at the counter and listen to the servers describe each of them in detail. Nothing better than getting to know what you put in your mouth.

Traditional Japanese cuisine is served in the restaurant's seasonal menu but they also serve some experimental dishes, for those feeling brave and brash. The Ginza Kojyu also has a decent wine list that will go exceptionally well with anything on the menu.

A usual menu in Ginza Kojyu would start with Tuskidashi (hors d'oeuvre), Owan (soup), Otsukuri (Sashimi), Yakinomo (Broiled fish & meats), Shokuji (Rice), and then dessert. The Kojyu has been awarded 3 stars from Michelin. Make sure to reserve your table in advance as many guests visit the small restaurant because of its relatively affordable menu. Located at Ginza, Chuo-ku, Tokyo, the restaurant is a 5-minute walk from the Tokyo Metro Ginza and a 3-minute walk from JR Shinbashi.

The Kojyu closed on Sundays and holidays. It is open from 5:30 PM to 12: AM from Monday to Friday and closes early at 9:30 PM on Saturdays. The price for course menu ranges from 15,000 yen to 25,000 yen and the restaurant accepts credit card payments.

New York Grill

Dining in a floor-to-ceiling glass window restaurant located on the 52nd floor of a building that has a stunning panorama of Tokyo and its skyline is an amazing experience. Located at the Park Hyatt Hotel, the restaurant is a mix of muted sophistication and modern interior design. It is best to ask for a table by the window so you can enjoy the breathtaking view. Menus include weekday lunch, brunch, dinner course, dinner ala carte, and dessert.

Are you all about meat? Then you will be tickled pink to know that you can choose from a wide assortment of seafood, poultry and the best prime quality cuts of beef, both imported and Japanese (especially Kobe Prime Cut and Hokkaido Ribeye).

The New York Grill has an extensive wine list, with its wine cellar brimming over with over 1,800 bottles of wine, you'll be sure to have the perfect bottle to go with your meals. The restaurant is open daily for lunch (11:30 AM to 2:30 PM) and dinner (5:30 PM and 10:00 PM) Reservations are required and you can book via phone or online.

Beard

Looking to experience Californian cuisine merged with Japanese culinary craftsmanship? Then visit the Beard for a casual, quiet yet fulfilling dining pleasure. The restaurant has only 12 seats, 4 in the counter and 8 in tables but it has become very popular since 2012 so you would need to make early reservations (several weeks ahead) and arrive early. The menu at the Beard regularly changes and it is inspired by seasonal local ingredients and imported ones.

The concept of the restaurant is slow food and preparation and cooking of the dishes are done with meticulousness while diners watch. Sunday brunches, priced usually around 2,000 yen includes homemade granola, avocado toast, and sourdough pancakes and the quite popular breakfast favourites at Beard.

Located at Meguro, Meguro-ko, you can get there via the Meguro Station. The restaurant is open from 5:30 PM to 12:00 midnight, Tuesdays to Saturday and 10:00 AM to 2:30 PM on Sundays.

Ivy Place

Relish European cuisine in a relaxing Asian environment. The Ivy Place is a popular restaurant among lunching ladies, especially those who bring their babies or pampered pups. Guests can enjoy a hefty breakfast of pancakes, egg dishes, granola, egg dishes and smoothies among other items on the menu. Soups, salads, and a selection of pasta sets are on the lunch menu. Diners can have dinner either in a relaxed room or at the bar counters. Dishes cost around 1,200 to 2,000 yen.

Located at Daikanyama T-Site, the Ivy Place is open from 7:00 AM to 10:45 AM for breakfast, 11:30 AM to 3:00 PM for lunch and 6:00 PM to 10:00 PM for dinner. Pancakes, are an all-day favourite, and are served from 7:00 AM to 5:00 PM. Reservations are recommended to ensure your seats at the rated 3 Michelin stars restaurant.

Sukiyabashi Jiro

This veteran sushi place serves some of the best sushi in Tokyo and is one of the best restaurants in Asia. The Sukiyabashi Jiro restaurant is simple and cozy and is able to serve 10 tables at a time. However, turnover of diners is timely so the flow of people in the restaurant is fairly good. Master Chef Jiro Ono believes that high-quality sushi should be prepared, served and consumed quickly to get the best experience. Guests would use their hands to eat sushi quickly, drink hot tea then leave the stall. It is quite hard to get into this restaurant but if you want to experience the expertise of Master Chef Jiro, then make the effort to get that reservation. It is good to note that the sushi is prepared based on your reservation time so don't be late. The tasting menu at Sukiyabashi consists of only 20 small courses. You can find Sukiyabashi Jiro at the Basement 1st floor of the Tsukamoto Sogyo Building in Chuo-ku, Tokyo.

Higashiyama

The food served in Higashiyama is as attractive as the stylish interior of the restaurant.

If you want to go for traditional Japanese dishes for lunch, you can enjoy steamed rice, seasonal fish, pickled veggies and usual miso soup. Higashiyama also serves extravagant dishes of duck, chicken and octopus for dinner. Guests who desire to have a nightcap can settle in the lounge downstairs where cocktails are served.

With modern furniture, calligraphy artwork and dimly lit corridors Higashiyama is a perfect picture of contemporary Japanese minimalist design. It is ideal to make reservations and you can take the Nakameguro Station to get there. Lunch menu costs around 3,000 yen while dinner menu price range is around 6,000 yen. The Higashimaya is open 11:30 AM to 3:00 PM from Tuesdays to Saturdays and 6:00 PM to 1:00 AM on Mondays.

Takazawa

Ever experienced what it would be like to feel like a guest of honor while dining? Then book that experience at the Takazawa, where there are only four tables and understand the real meaning of specialized. Let Chef Takazawa and his wife serve you and let you enjoy savory dishes served innovatively. The setting is very private and guests will enjoy watching the chef masterfully prepare their dining fares. Guests who dine here say that it is such a culinary delight and don't mind paying a little bit extra given the unique and personalized experience it gives back in return.

It is a little challenging to get a reservation at Takazawa, owing testament to its wide, year-round popularity amongst regulars and locals, but it is well worth it because this is one restaurant that is off the charts! Takazawa is located at the Sanyo Akasaka Building in Akasaka, Minato-ku.

Sushi Saito

This 3-Michelin star restaurant is known the world over, amongst food enthusiasts and travel foodies, as one of the best, if not the best, sushi restaurant in the world. Like most other notable restaurants in Tokyo, it only has eight seats so you have to make a reservation many weeks in advance. Sushi Saito is one of the World's 50 Best Restaurants, and the clamor for seats attest to the unique experience of fresh ingredients coupled with that personal touch of the gracious chefs and staff.

Guests are a little surprised at the tiny space the restaurant is housed, but this quickly melts away upon understanding the personalized service the experience brings. Guests will be delighted to know that the dishes are prepared using only the finest, freshest and best ingredients to ensure that your taste buds and stomachs are satiated.

The talented and multi-skilled food styling of Chef Takashi Saito will make sure that there is a balance of flavor, texture and temperature in everything he serves. The relaxed restaurant serves many high-quality dishes but the most popular are squid and tuna. Enjoy different cuts of mackerel, tuna, eel, sea urchin and octopus from the procession of meticulously prepared, hand-crafted sushi. Quite uncommon in other sushi restaurants, Chef Saito serves the sushi with freshly grated wasabi; lemon and soy sauce instead of letting the diners make their own dip. You can find Sushi Saito at the Ark Hills Tower in Minato, Tokyo.

Some Tips When Dining in Japan

The best thing about traveling is getting a taste of the local cuisine. Make sure you understand Japan's rules, manners and services before you dine so you don't make an unfortunate cultural mistake. Here are some things you need to remember:

- Tipping is not required. In fact, it is quite insulting in Japanese culture.

- In Japanese taverns, you will be served otoshi or tsukidashi even if you don't ask for it. Naturally, it will be added to your bill.

- Water is always served free. Some restaurants even offer hot tea.

- When you eat at izakaya, sushi and yakiniku restaurants, all-you-can-eat and all-you-can drink services are fairly common and offered at a reasonable price.

- Wet towels or osibori that you can use to wipe your hands or mouth are offered individually to customers at no charge.

- Food and drinks from the "outside" are not allowed, except in food courts in shopping malls.

Chapter Six: Shopping in Tokyo

It's almost impossible to think of Tokyo without thinking "shopping" too. How can it be possible, right? Being in the midst of the source of futuristic technology, and with us up to our elbows in it with everyday life, how can we not? Trip the light fantastic as you stroll along electrified streets of miles and miles of where the production of everything you can dream up has probably been made.

Whether you are going for high-end fashion, second-hand treasures, souvenirs, vintage items, merchandise toys, or traditional crafts, you will surely find it in the many stores in the city. With a number of flagship stores, boutiques, department stores, discount stores and used select shops — Tokyo's vibrant retail landscape is like no other! Here is a list of the top 10 places to shop in Tokyo to help you plan a unique shopping experience on your trip. Don't forget to duck into the smaller shops that you will surely find

Shibuya Shopping District

Easily the most popular shopping place in Tokyo, Shibuya is home to many places for shopping, recreation and entertainment.

Shibuya 109: Shibuya takes the cake for teen trendiness in Japan, and Shibuya 109 is the heart of teen fashion in the district. It is easy to spot as it is housed in an iconic, and hard-to-miss 10-storey, high-rise building. One can't help but be amazed at the amount of trendy apparel, stylish shoes, beauty products, elaborate accessories, branded makeup, costumes, and other youth-focused fashion items that are available.

Tokyu Hands: In the mood for shopping for your hobby, lifestyle, and home improvement? Visit Tokyu Hands for stationery, art supplies and DIY craft projects. The 8-storey shop in Shibuya, the biggest and first in Japan, also offers travel items, outdoor equipment, gadgets and interior accessories.

United Arrows & Sons: Classier gentlemen may want to drop by United Arrows & Sons; an iconic store offers a great selection of modern tailoring and classic menswear.

The Real McCoys: For men who go for the classic outfitter or military bunker look, it's time to get a crewneck and M-65 jacket from The Real McCoys.

Bounty Hunter: Looking for pop culture collectibles and comic books as well as apparel that are released with them?

Then drop by the Bounty Hunter for great finds.

Many flagship stores such as White Mountaineering, Supreme, and Free International Library (FIL) can also be found in the Shibuya District. The not-so-adventurous in fashion can always shop in the familiar, well-known international brands H&M and Forever 21. You can also score great finds from many independent stores, smaller shops and 100 Yen discount shops when you traverse inner roads and alleyways in the district.

Ginza

If you are up for shopping for some luxury items and local products, you should visit the posh boutiques and high-end department stores that are lined up at glitzy Ginza. The Ginza Mitsukoshi is the oldest Japanese department store which features everything you can think of and caters to men, women and children of all sizes and ages. Shop for high quality toys, clothes, and housewares as you go through its seven floors and don't forget to visit the restaurant for some delicious Japanese cuisine.

Tokyu Plaza Ginza: Check out the latest high-fashion mall opened in 2016 to score some popular Japanese brands and prominent world brands.

Dover Street Market: The avant-garde store is a must-visit for shoppers in Tokyo.

Ginza Hakuhinkan Toy Park: This toy shop offers adventure for all ages. Be sure to check out their Mini-4WD track and have some fun.

Itōya: Discover floors and floors of art supplies and beautiful stationery, cards, crafts and Japanese gadgets. Sanrio World: Hello, Hello Kitty fans! This is a shop you definitely must visit. Get presents for our friends from the biggest Sanrio product shop in the whole world or buy yourself a souvenir!

Yurakucho Marui: This is the shop for the younger generation where they can find high quality fashion items at reasonable prices.

Neighborhood Stores: You will also enjoy shopping for crafts at Takumi as well as gourmet food items at Akoymeya.

Kōenji and Kichijōji: The old-fashioned yet very appealing suburbs found in western Tokyo, Kōenji and Kichijōji are just 10 minutes away from each other. Kichijōji is a haven for people who love housewares and zakka while Kōenji is known for shops that sell vintage clothing and second-hand items.

Kōenji

Kita-Kore Building: Kita-Kore in a variety of fashion stores for many trendy finds.

Sokkyō: The store is easy to miss so make sure you ask around to check it out for highly sought-after vintage goods. Other stores where you can get vintage clothing include Yakusoku, Mouse, Kissmet, Laugh, JuRian, and Sokkyou. In Kichijōji, Outbound: This is one of the best places to get boho objects.

Markus: Feast your eyes on pottery, kitchenware and handmade fans and be sure to have enough money as you will be tempted to splurge.

Puku Puku: Buy beautiful antique ceramics for your home or as gifts from this store.

Kuramae

This former warehouse district is now a budding place for young artisans and shops that carry one-of-a-kind goods.

Camera: Bask in (Numeri) handmade leather goods even as you enjoy (Miwako Bake) yummy delicacies and smoothies.

Kakimori: Experience crafting your own ink colour and designing a notebook in this shop.

Maito: Enjoy warm and calm colors as you shop here for traditionally and naturally dyed clothes.

Carmine: Looking for a unique accessory? Everything handcrafted at Carmine has a characteristic design that will surely catch your fancy.

Asakusa

Enjoy traditional street food, souvenir trinkets, novelty items and more at the Asukasa neighbourhood.

Nakamise-dōri: Walk along the many alleyways and smaller lanes to get high quality trinkets, handicrafts, sweets and fabrics that you can bring home to friends and family.

Hisago-dori: You won't be able to resist wagashi (a traditional Japanese confection) even as you go around shopping for kimonos and getas (wooden sandals).

Denbouin-dori: This is the place to get handcrafted Japanese fans, high-quality kiriko (cut glass) and other antiques.

Don Quijote: If you somehow forgot to get souvenirs and you're bound to go home the next day, then go to Don Quixote and get super discounts on so many different Japanese items.

More stores: Get culinary supplies at Kappabashi-dōri, noren at Bengara, arts and crafts items at Marugoto Nippon, and vintage items at Tokyo Hotarudo.

Shimo-Kitazawa

Both tourists and locals visit the small neighborhood that is famous for hole-in-the-wall bars and quirky shops. If you are the arty kind of person, then go on a culture trip at Shimokita.

Haight & Ashbury: One of the best, high-end vintage-clothing shops in Tokyo. You can get 19th and 20th century vintage items and other one-of-a-kind quality articles.

Ocean BLVD: Score some quirky finds—vintage, handmade and unique second-hand clothes.

Chicago: This is a popular place to buy kimonos, yukatas, obi and other Japanese clothing accessories as well as many vintage finds.

Harajuku and Aoyama

Take a stroll along the peaceful and pleasant districts of Harajuku and Aoyama, lined with trendy stores and chic restaurants. Omotesando is the most popular shopping street here.

Kiddyland: If you are travelling (and shopping) with your kids, then visit this emporium located along Omotesando where they can purchase kawaii characters and other kinds of toys.

Oriental Bazaar: Buy first-class souvenirs and Japanese arts and crafts from this giant store as keepsake or gifts.

Fuji-Torii: Don't forget to check out beautiful Japanese antiques and arts in this small store along Omotesando.

Omotesando Hills: This high fashion store is one of the most expensive boutiques in Tokyo.

Laforet: You will notice youthful fashion as you traverse Omotesando. Popular with trendy youth but not high-end, you can find similar items at the boutiques in Laforet.

Akihabara

If you are looking for Japanese electronics, go to Akihabara Electric Town District—Tokyo's electronic hub. It is also popular shopping place for otakus who fancy J-pop, anime, manga and retro video games. There are hundreds of electronics shops including Akihabara Radio Center, Yodobashi Electronics Store, Sofmap, Laox, Yodabashi Camera, and the Akihabara Crossfield. Otakus will love to visit the Maid Café, Radio Kaikan, Gamers, Super Potato, Don Quijote, Mandarake and the Tsukumo Robot Kingdom.

Other stores you will find are 2k540 Aki-Oka Artisan, a crafts bazaar, and Jimbōchō which houses 170 bookstores.

Daikanyama and Naka-Meguro

Want to feel more like a citizen rather than a tourist? Explore the chic cafes and stylish shops at Daikanyama and Naka-Meguro.

1LDK Apartments: The clothing store offers a selection for men and women, as well as a variety of food and housewares.

Tsutaya Books: The happy place for booklovers, Tsutaya boasts of an impressive—and seemingly bottomless— collection of books and magazines.

Giraffe Daikanyama Hillside Terrace: Express yourself with unique and all-original ties: classic, skinny, bolo and bow ties. Giraffe also has a great necklace section for ladies.

Have A Good Time: The store sells fashion pieces that promote cool art and street culture. You can get creative tees, sweat tops and other accessories.

J'Antiques: Score modish vintage American clothing, antique accessories, and furniture from as early as the 1800s.

Shinjuku

Shinjuku is bustling with activity because of the many malls and department stores. It can be a great choice for those who like one-stop shopping; you can find something for everybody. The district is divided into three: South, East and West of the station.

West: Here you can find electronics shops, big department stores, and major hotels.

South: The place to get chic mid-range to high-end fashion items.

East: This is the part of the district where there are many dining opportunities as well as high-class shopping. Popular department stores include Isetan, Shinjuku Odakyu Department Store, HALC, Keio Department Store, Lumine and Shinjuku MYLORD.

Shinjuku Flags: This retail store specializes in sporting goods, music and fashion items carry brands such as Tower Records, Gap, Oshman's, and Camper.

Here are some tips that can make your shopping experience even more enjoyable:

- You can take advantage of tax refunds for purchases meant for personal use.

- Remember to bring your passport and check out the stores that have tax-free stickers on their windows.

- Keep all your receipts and original packaging as you may need it in making declarations at the airport when you go home.

- When shopping in Tokyo, it is best to carry cash. Despite modernity, Japanese culture frowns upon the use of credit cards. Spending cash that you actually have is encouraged so you will find some small stores and traditional ones do not have credit payment facilities.

- While bargaining may be a custom in Asia, it is only done at Japanese flea markets and not in shopping districts.

Shopping can make you hungry, or you may want to buy food items as gifts. Don't forget to visit the food halls located at the basement of many of Tokyo's department stores.

Chapter Seven: Tourist Spots in Tokyo

Tokyo is a city that has a lot to offer in terms of tourist attractions and entertainment. You can start your day by having a sushi breakfast at the world-renowned Tsukiji Fish Market then delve into interesting Japanese history, take on the massive shopping scene, visit traditional sites, or unwind in lush gardens. Tokyo is a city that has a lot to offer in terms of tourist attractions and entertainment.

You can start your day by having breakfast sushi at the world-renowned Tsukiji Fish Market then delve into interesting Japanese history, take on the massive shopping scene, visit traditional sites, or unwind in lush gardens. Here are ten of the top tourist destinations you can go to when your visit Tokyo:

Tokyo Disneyland

The magic is here! Disneyland is not just for children, it is for the child-at-heart. Whether you are travelling alone or with your family, make sure to book tickets to Disneyland and experience this enchanted kingdom where dreams come true. The theme park is popular for its wide open spaces that can accommodate big crowds. There are many rides and attractions you can visit, most of them based on Disney films and fantasies. Some of the most famous ones are:

World Bazaar: Omnibus, Penny Arcade

Adventure Land: Pirates of the Caribbean, Swiss Family Treehouse and Jungle Cruise: Wildlife Expeditions, Western River Railroad

Tomorrowland: Star Tours, Buzz Lightyear's Astro Blasters, Monsters Inc. Hide n' Go Seek, Space Mountain

Western Land: Countrybear Theater, Westernland Shooting Gallery, Mark Twain Riverboat, Big Thunder Mountain, Tom Sawyer Island Rafts

Critter Country: Beaver Brothers Exploration Canoe, Splash Mountain

Fantasyland: Cinderella's Fairytale Halls, Castle Carousel, Alice's Tea Party, It's a Small World, Snow White's Adventures, Peter Pan's Flight

Toontown: Goofy's Paint and Play House, Chip n' Dale's Treehouse, Toon Park, Minnie's House

Tokyo Disneyland is a happy place, a source of imagination, fun, and laughter that visitors can enjoy, whether they are traveling by themselves or with loved ones.

Tokyo Sea Life Park

Located across Tokyo Disneyland, this is another must-go attraction for the whole family. If you love marine

environments and all things related to the ocean world, you shouldn't miss going to the Sea Life Park, which is open from 9:30 AM to 5:00 PM. Let your kids see, learn about and appreciate diverse sea life. Not only will guests be awed at the amazing creatures than can be found in the world's waters, they will also be made aware of the importance of caring for and preserving marine life. The Tokyo Sea Life Park is a well-built and beautifully designed aquarium that displays plentiful habitats from the Atlantic Ocean, Indian Ocean, Caribbean Sea and of course, Tokyo Bay.

- You can see a wide variety of fish from different regions around the world.
- Guests get to meet penguins, turtles, puffins, bamboo sharks, and stingrays.
- The entrance to the park is a massive glass dome on the edge of the water and you get a great view of Tokyo Bay.
- It is open daily from 9:30 AM to 5:00 PM except on Wednesdays.

The Imperial Palace

Tokyo is the official residence of the Emperor of Japan and the Imperial family. The Imperial Palace is in the Chiyoda ward where the private abode of the family, as well as administrative offices, museums and an archive is situated. The Imperial Palace was home to many important figures and rulers of Japan including Emperor Meiji. However, famous and rich in tradition as it is, you won't see it mobbed by tourists even though it is clearly a place worth visiting. Since it is the home of the imperial family, a visit to see the Imperial Palace is subject to an application policy. Visitors would need to send in an application a few weeks ahead of time to gain get admittance.

Applications are not easy, but it is well worth the effort. However, once you get permission to visit, you have to understand that access inside the palace is limited.

- Palace tours are scheduled at 10:00 AM and 1:30 PM.

- If you prefer not to get put in an application for a physical walk through of the palace, you can always admire the palace from afar. It is a breathtaking structure considering the clout of the residents

The East Gardens in the complex, open to the public, is a very attractive sight of lush green spaces and shady spots. It is also very beautiful during cherry blossom season. The East Gardens are open to visitors from 9:00 AM to 4:30 PM.

Tokyo National Museum

A lot of travelers love discovering about the history of the places they go visit. If you are one such traveler, you can learn more about the roots and traditions of this great country through thousands of artifacts and art pieces carefully curated and displayed in the Tokyo National Museum. Among about 116,000 pieces that cover most of Japan's history, some of them considered national treasures; you will find unique relics such as:

- samurai swords

- samurai armors

- delicate pottery

- kimonos

- paintings

- calligraphy

You can learn more about a country and its people when you visit their museums. In the Tokyo National Museum, you can also find other artifacts from all across Asia. English translations are featured, making it easy for visitors to appreciate the displays. You can easily reach the museum via the metro and it is best to enjoy a full day inside it.

Afterwards, you can check out the rest of Ueno Park. Next to the Ueno Station in Central Tokyo, Ueno Park is Japan's first ever Western-styled park. Visit the Shinobazu Pond, Bentedo temple hall, and of course, Ueno Zoo, the first zoological garden of the country.

Tokyo National Museum of Emerging Science and Innovation

Popularly known as the Miraikan, this museum is a testament to Tokyo's proclivity to innovation, science and technology, and entrepreneurship. If you want to get a glimpse of emerging technology in Japan, check out this museum—it will be worth your time.

There are many high-tech, interactive displays among the three themed exhibits:

- Explore the Frontiers: an autographed model of the International Space Station can be seen.

- Discover Your Earth: a large sculpture of the earth on a LED panel will allow you to appreciate our planet even more.

- Create Your Future: get a glimpse of Honda's ASIMO robot in this exhibit.

- Children will love the displays as they can play with, touch and even climb on them.

Science workshops and talks happen at different times in the museum and at the GAIA 3D Home Theater. The museum is open from 10:00 AM to 5:00 PM.

Tokyo Metropolitan Government Building

Tokyo's cityscape is one of the most beautiful in the world. Take a free trip to the Metropolitan Government Tower and get a bird's eye view of the city. The Metropolitan Government Tower is a 202-meter skyscraper that houses two observatories that give visitors the highest vantage points and 360-degree views.

- Enjoy watching a magical sunset at the observatory and even see Mt. Fuji if you are lucky to check it out on a clear day.

- The North Observatory is open from 9:30 AM to 11:00 PM while the South Observatory closes at 5:30 PM.

- There is no time restriction for visits to the building and you will enjoy speedy elevators, few lines and very accommodating customer service.

While admission costs you no money, you may want to bring cash to enjoy the plentiful dining options available.

Shinjuku Gyoen National Garden

Enjoy a picnic at the gorgeously landscaped Shinjuku Gyoen National Garden. Choose from any of the three differently themed spots: Traditional Japanese, English Garden and French Formal. The 144 acres of lush space lined with cherry blossoms during spring is a very popular attraction for tourists and locals alike. Take a stroll or sit down for a picnic and revel in the calm atmosphere that the park exudes. There are many amenities such as dining places, teahouse, greenhouse and restrooms all over the park for guests to enjoy. Open from Tuesday to Sunday, you can get in the park for a minimal fee of 200 yen.

Tokyo Tower

More than just an attraction or an eyesore, depending on your perspective, the Tokyo Tower, the Japanese "homage" to France's Eiffel Tower is also a broadcasting structure that supports 62 miles of radio and television frequencies. There are two observation decks that provide tourists an awesome view of the cityscape. One is 490 feet high and the other is 819 feet into the air.

You can enjoy tea while admiring the stunning vistas in the Tower's café and you can also get souvenirs at their on-site shops. Open from 9:00 AM to 11:00 PM, admission is 900 yen for adults and 350 yen for children 4 years old and below. While you can go any time of the day, the best time to visit the Tokyo Tower is at night.

Ghilbi Museum

Are you a fan of anime and all things fantastic and whimsical? Then you must visit the Ghilbi Museum which features the amazing work of Hayao Miyazaki's Studio Ghilbi.

- The designs and exhibits are not formal but quirky because it depicts the animation studio.

- Children can have fun in a play area that even has a life-sized Cat Bus.

- The museum has many books in the reading room and a rooftop garden where you can see sculptures of different characters.

- If you are a Miyazaki fan, you wouldn't mind the extra effort in securing tickets to the Ghilbi Museum to experience this magical world.

- The museum is open from 10:00 AM to 6:00 PM from Wednesday to Monday.

- You must purchase tickets in advance as you cannot get them from the museum.

- It is accessible via the JR Chou Line in the Mitaka Station.

Tsukiji Market

Most tourists will go to shopping centers or flea markets but other travelers prefer food markets. And if you are one such lover of food, specifically seafood, Tsukiji Market is the place to get an unforgettable experience. It is located right in the middle of Central Tokyo.

Sushi connoisseurs should never pass up the chance to check out the the Tsukiji market. About 500 different kinds of seafood are sold here — from the basic tuna to the exotic sea urchin.

- Sushi stalls line up the market where you can get the freshest fish.

- If you are not keen on seafood, you can check out the stalls that sell other produce.

- There are also restaurants that serve different meals, such as the Mosuke Dango where you can get sweet dumplings, Indo Curry or some curry, and other restaurants for some delicious cuisine.

- The market is busy every day except on Wednesdays and Sundays.

- Keep in mind that children are not allowed here because the market is always dense with people and robustly eventful.

For all its many attractions, most travelers will say that just being in Tokyo is enough. It is one of the safest cities in the world where you will meet English-speaking students who are always ready to offer help and answer your questions. So book that trip now to experience the magical land that is the City of Tokyo.

Chapter Eight: Tokyo Shrines and Temples

Tokyo, Japan is a popular destination for travelers for so many reasons: Michelin-Star restaurants, high-end fashion shops, nightlife, and five-star hotels among others. But if you are looking for an authentic Japanese experience, there is no better way than to visit the temples and shrines in the city. Sensoji Temple (also known as the Asakusa Kannon Temple). Founded in 628 A.D, the Sensoji is the oldest temple in Tokyo and is the main temple of the Sho-Kannon sect. The temple and shrine grounds are open all day, every day and visitors can come in for free.

Kaminarimon Gate: It is the colossal, red, outermost gate of the temple that is usually the first stop of a tourist visiting **Asakusa:** Highly photographed, the giant red chocin lantern characterizes this popular spot.

Nakamise dori: Along the bustling shopping street that leads to the temple, you can get different kinds of souvenir trinkets, crafts and snacks. Hozonmon Gate is the second gate in front of the temple hall. Twice the size of Kaminarimon, a huge paper lantern and two gigantic waraji hang on it. The Kannondo Hall is the main building of the temple, built in 1651 and rebuilt after World War II. There is a golden image of Kannon, the Goddess of Mercy, believed to be in the hall. The five-story Goju-no-To Pagoda is also a sight to see. There is a tea garden beside it, but it is closed to the public.

The Asakusa Shrine: located at the right of the temple, this is dedicated to the three fishermen who discovered Kannon's golden image in the 7th century.

If you visit in May, you will get to experience the loudest and grandest festival in Tokyo, Sanja Matsuri.

Meiji-Jingu Shrine

A very stately shrine, the Meiji-Jingu is surrounded by the beautiful expanse of lush greens that is the Yoyogi Park.

Some amazing facts about the shrine include the following:

- The shrine was built to venerate Emperor Meiji, the first constitutional monarch who played a crucial role on the modernization of Japan.
- There is a museum that stores the historical memorabilia of Emperor Meiji and his wife Empress Shoken as well as their court.
- There are over a hundred thousand trees that surround the shrine and you can explore the woods through the walkways.
- The shrine is quite busy during New Year as millions of patrons visit at this time.

You may even get to see a traditional Japanese wedding when you visit the shrine as it is a popular venue for such.

Tennoji Temple

Looking for a temple with a unique location? Tennoji Temple is set in the middle of a wood-like cemetery lined with a long landscape of cherry trees. Tennoji embodies tranquility as it is enhanced by nature. The temple, which is over 800 years old, is surrounded by landscaped boroughs and lawns and a modern-looking gate .There is an impressive bronze Buddha in the main lawn to welcome you into the centre of the site. While at present it exudes quietude, you will be surprised to know that once upon a time in history, it was the place where they used to hold Tokyo's largest public lottery!

Yasukuni Shrine

Looking for a temple with a unique location? Tennoji Temple is set in the middle of a wood-like cemetery lined with a long landscape of cherry trees. Tennoji embodies tranquility as it is enhanced by nature. The temple, which is over 800 years old, is surrounded by landscaped boroughs and lawns and a modern-looking gate. The shrine is more political than religious as it is devoted to Japan's war dead.

- There are many memorials and statues related to war, as well as a war museum.

- Located at Kudanzaka slope and in very close proximity to the Imperial Palace, Yasukuni Shrine is one of the landscapes that define Tokyo City.

- Visit on weekends and shop at second-hand markets. Visit oin July to join the Mitama Matsuri festivals.

Koganji Temple

The Koganji Temple is visited by locals and tourists because of the Jigo Togenuki believed to possess healing properties. The temple is always open and visitors can come in for free all the time. To get healing for any part of their body, visitors pour water over the corresponding part of the Jizo Togenuki, an all-black Bodhisattva. You can reach the temple by walking—it is only 8 minutes away from the Sugamo Station.

Akagi Shrine

The Akagi is one of the most modern shrines in Tokyo built on top of Kagurazaka Hill.

This is not your usual Japanese Shrine. Architect Kengo Kuma directed its renewal in 2010 and the shrine has become a modern Shinto holy site. You will find a lot of recurring flea markets around it as well as a museum gallery and casual Italian restaurant, Akagi Cafe. It is easy to reach, merely a 4-minute walk from the Kagurazaka Station.

Nezu Shrine

Want to visit a shrine that has 2,000 years of Japanese history? The beautiful Nezu Shrine is the memorial most closely associated with the Imperial family as well as Shogun doings.

It is one of the oldest and most picturesque shrines in Japan. Legends say that the Nezu Shrine was first instituted in Sendagi by Prince Osu ("Yamato Takeru") a fearsome leader who lived in the first century A.D.

- The Nezu Shrine was transferred to the Nezu area in the 17th century in commemoration of Shogun Tsunayoshi Tokugawa choosing of a successor.

- Renowned for the lush greenery and its azalea garden, you can bask in the shrine's vibrant spring colors of white, purple and pink at Nezu Shrine as well as ponds of carp.

- The shrine also has tastefully designed old buildings that show off traditional Japanese designs.

- Take a picture at the hundreds of beautiful torii arches around the gorgeous

Yushima Seido Temple

This is the temple that expresses the role of Chinese Confucianism has in Japan. The Yushima Seido Temple was founded by Hayashi Razan, a neo-Confucian scholar who taught the first four shoguns. It was formerly located in the area now known as Ueno Park.

- Yushima literally means "sacred hall". In 1690, it was transferred to Bunkyo ward in Tokyo by Tokugawa and was authorized as the training center for Shogun bureaucrats in the 18th century.

- The temple plays an important role in the education system of Japan and was the site for many education-related institutions. Students consider the Yushima Seido a place of supplication.

- Yushima Seido has the largest Confucius statue in the world.

- The temple is a testament to the important contribution of Chinese history to the modern life of Japan.

Narita-san Fukagawa Fudo-Do Temple

Experience the extreme contrasts of old world tradition and ultra - modernity in the temple popularly called Fukagawa Fudoson. Smack dab in the middle of modern Tokyo, the richly historical and traditional structure houses a deep history of the old Tokyo which spans over centuries of tradition. Imagine what it must have been like in the ancient days and dive into a centuries old tradition of blessing your possessions. One can be immersed and be part of the purification ritual at the Fukagawa Fudoson which would include wafting your personal belongings over burning cedar sticks. In order to be part of this long tradition, pay the fee in order to join one of the scheduled rituals which take place five times a day. Fukagawa Fudoson can be found on 1 Chome-17-13 Tomioka, Tokyo 135-0047 and is in close proximity to other noteworthy and attractive temples.

Yushima Tenjin Shrine

Only 10 minutes north of Yushima Seido, Yushima

Tenjin is situated on 3 Chome-30-1 Yushima, Bunkyō, Tokyo

113-0034. The Yushima Tenjin is a scenic shrine dedicated to

the Shinto god, Ameno-tajikarao no-mikoto. The Shrine was

also once associated with Sugawara no Michizane, a classical

Confucian sage. You will be greeted by what locals call the

"stroking ox" outside of the shrine. The stroking ox is a

locally known as a "nadeshi" and it is made of bronze that is

believed to bring healing. The magnificently made,

picturesque building is constructed out of golden brown cedar and is detailed with vivid carvings and mesmerizing frescoes. It is not unusual for students, looking for divine help and intervention, to visit the Yushima Tenjin shrine because it deified Sugawara, venerated as the god of learning.

Most of the temples and shrines in Tokyo have been reconstructed in modern times because of the destruction caused them when these shrines and temples were bombed, raided or burned down during the Second World War. Despite the more sturdy materials used and the obvious upgraded bits that goes with the building modernity of today, one would still be able to experience the expansive, rich history and long standing traditions that is the heart of the temples and shrines of Tokyo. A visit to Tokyo is it is worth it to check them out when you go to the city.

Chapter Nine: Nightlife in Tokyo

Tokyo is home to countless clubs, bars, and drinking spots. The capital of Japan is quite alive and bustling when night falls. With all the dazzling lights, neon skyscrapers and an irresistible energy that attracts many people to the night life it is no wonder why it is touted to be a city that never seems to sleep. From simple spots where you can enjoy cocktails, wine, sake, craft beer and other drink options to more lavish lounges and upscale bars, you can expect to have an unforgettable and exciting time. The nightlife in Tokyo is legendary. This chapter will cover the top 10 spots you shouldn't dare miss!

Robot Restaurant

Experience a night like no other at the Shinjuku Robot Restaurant where you will see futuristic robots, lasers, drums, special effects and high-energy dancer's party the night away. If you are game for a Japanese cabaret show, then you will enjoy the one-hour shows at the Robot Restaurant. Very close to the Shinjuku Station, the Robot Restaurant is located at the Kabuchiko district and is one of the most visited nightlife spots in Tokyo. You won't find this experience anywhere else in the world.

The musical shows will give you a sensory overload of designs, color, flashing lights, and glitter. You will be entertained, amazed, or even baffled. But you will surely have an amazing time seeing the incredible performances of glitzy girls dancing with dinosaurs, ninjas, samurais, giant pandas to the beat of techno music and taiko drums. Since it has gained popularity over the years, the shows at the Robot restaurant have become family-friendly and the sexuality and violence have either been toned down or removed.

If you are bringing kids, go to the first two shows on a weekday. Ticket prices include a discount drink but no food. You can choose among sake, beer, soft drink or mineral water. You can pre-order a bento box, snacks and other drinks that you also pay in advance. You can also have a photo op with the robots. Be sure to arrive forty minutes early as you will not be allowed to go in and your ticket will not be refunded or rescheduled.

Bar High Five

One of the most respected and highly popular bars in Ginza is High Five. While the bar is not big and allows room for 10 bar seats, High Five has a wide selection of more than 200 bottles of scotch and whiskey and offers amazing cocktails.

Bar High Five doesn't have a menu though, a staff will ask you about your tastes and offer a suggestion then prepare you a personalized beverage you will surely enjoy. There is no food served except for fruit but you can enjoy a selection of amuse bouche. Bar High Five is a more popular

spot for couples instead of groups, especially with the slow
jazz background music that usually welcomes people after
dinner. Experience this bar's old-style charm at the 4t Floor
of the Polestar Building in Ginza, Chuo-ko.

Brooklyn Parlor

When you just want a place to relax after you've had
a long, tiring day of shopping or sightseeing, go to the
Brooklyn Parlor and rest your feet and back on a
comfortable armchair and enjoying a good glass of wine or

cold beer. During the day, the Brooklyn Parlor is a hip coffee shop that is a popular go-to place for students. At night, it draws a dynamic crowd that enjoys house and techno music performed by DJs. You can munch on chargrilled burgers and pancakes as you surf the internet or go through their large selection of books. You can get Brooklyn Lager beer on tap. The bar is open from 11:30 AM to 11:30 PM. Take the Shinjuku Station to go to the Brooklyn Parlor nestled at B1F Shinjuku Marui Annex.

AgeHa

This is the largest and most popular nightclub in Tokyo and has the best sound system in the city. AgeHa boasts of three dance floors, an abundance of areas for guests to chill, a pool area, open terrace, outdoor dance tent, several numbers of bars and VIP rooms. The main dancefloor, Area, can accommodate up to 2,400 guests. World-renowned DJs have played music at AgeHa, such as

Fatboy Slim, Deep Dish, David Guetta, Markus Schulz, Hernan Cattaneo, Numanoid and Yasutaka Nakata of Capsule. Every other month, AgeHa hosts Shangri-la, a gay dance event.

You would be required to present an ID that will show you are of legal age before you are allowed entrance. If you are coming from central Tokyo, you can get a free 30-minute shuttle ride to Shin-Kiba to get to AgeHa.

Mandarin Bar

The stylish and luxurious Mandarin Bar is the perfect place to meet up with your friends and chill through the night. Grab an early evening aperitif then enjoy a sumptuous dinner of specialty dishes and delicacies. You can also go you can go after dinner and listen to jazz bands. The bar is famous for its spacious Zen interior and designer furnishings. Since the ambiance of the bar is that of a 5-star hotel, guests are often business people and women who like to enjoy excellent service. Make sure to try the Mandarin Bar signature Mancino Sakura & Sumire vermouth.

The Mandarin Bar is open from 11:30 Am to 2:00 AM, Mondays to Saturdays. The bar is located at the 37th floor of the Mandarin Oriental, a stunning high-rise in Nihonbashi , which is accessible via the Mitsukoshimae Station. If you are planning the ultimate date experience with a loved one, get dinner and champagne by the tables near the windows.

Ben Fiddich

Opting for a laidback cocktail lounge for the night? Drop by Ben Fiddich and be treated to a relaxing, peaceful night filled with traditional music. You will delight in the exclusive feel of this club as it only has 15 seats and is dimly lit. Meet world-famous Hiroyasu Kayama, an expert bartender who prefers to make spirits using homegrown plants, spices, herbs and fruits and a terracotta mortar and pestle.

Prepare to be amazed; with gin, whiskey, amaro and absinthe as the four basic spirits of Ben Fiddich's drinks, Kayama will prepare you cocktails that are totally off-the-cuff.star Tokyo bartender who has been heralded worldwide. Since 2013, Kayama's fascination with the way the natural world—plants, spices, fruits—and liquor dance together has led him to break apart and rebuild spirits and liqueurs from the ground up (amaro and Campari, to name a couple) using herbs that he grows on his family farm on the outskirts of Tokyo. Ben Fiddich, the most radical bar in Tokyo, is located at Nishi-Shinjuku.

GoodBeer Faucets

Right smack in the heart of the bustling Shibuya District, you can get great draft beers at GoodBeer Faucets, both international and Japanese. They have a state-of-the art beer tap system and offers the best if not the largest selection of craft beers in Tokyo. During happy hour, you can get pints at less than 200 yen. Don't forget to try their chai beer. GoodBeer is a spacious concrete craft beer room that is a good palce to get your drinks and spend the night away.

The bar is open from 5:00 PM to 8:00 PM, Mondays to Thursdays and 1:00 PM to 7:00 PM on Sundays. GoodBeer Faucets is situated at the 2nd floor of the Shibuya Crossroad Building.

Meishu Center Tokyo-Sake Tasting Bar

If you want to venture into the Japanese drinking experience, then go over to Meishu Center for a selection of over 500 variations of Japanese rice wine. Sourced from small individual traders all over the country, sake flavors offered at Meishu Center include lychee, banana, melon, plum and pear, among others. This is not a bar with a rowdy crowd, but a laid-back one. People who want to wind down after a day of shopping, going around or a long flight will enjoy the good vibe of this bar. The bar is lined with bottles and bottles of sake.

You choose one and a staff will give you a 60ml sample. You can drink as many sets as you want, just try not to get drunk. When you finally find one that you prefer, you can buy a bottle. You can also get snacks. You can choose from jerky, mackerel, boar meat, daikon, moray and different kinds of cheeses. These snack bits serve to enhance sake flavors and should be eaten while drinking. The Meishu Center is located at the first floor of Isoyama Dai-2 Building in Minato.

Genius

This is an upscale bar for people who don't want to hang out with youth, tourists or expats. The subtle setting is good to enjoy Japanese nightlife and you can enjoy high-end, formal partying. Get the VIP experience at Genius. It is a luxurious club located alongside upscale boutiques and is a 5-minute walk from Yurakutyo Station. Genius is a visually exciting and respectable club with great heart-thumping music and amazing drinks. Very casual clothing is frowned upon at Genius as Ginza is a business district.

Men are usually dapper but dress shirts over chinos are okay. Women don stylish dresses. Make sure you dress up so you won't be turned away at the door.

Gaspanic

For locals and tourists who want to meet foreigners and make new friends, Gaspanic is the club to go to. You won't feel too out of place even if it is your first time to the city and you speak little to no Japanese. Gaspanic is a melting pot of diverse cultures and you can easily blend in.

The vibe in Gaspanic is not pretentious and you can enjoy EDM and mainstream club music. You don't have to worry about entrance fees and they serve inexpensive drinks, only 800 yen per cocktail. So if you want to experience a bit of Tokyo nightlife but don't want to bother yourself with too much preparation or worry about costs, then Gaspanic is your best choice. Gaspanic is located at the Fuji Building in Shibuya.

Tokyo is one of the cities that never sleep. They have some of the best night clubs and bars worldwide. So whether you prefer rock, jazz, techno, house, or K-pop, Tokyo is a place where you can dance and drink the night away.

Chapter Ten:

Last Minute Traveller Tips

The city metropolis of Tokyo is indeed an eclectic city with a long history that has intermingled with the modern trappings of life and the sensibilities of today's lifestyle. It is an unconventional city that is a class of its own because of the many unexpected things to see and do here. If you are looking to do something a little more adventurous, that is away from the typical trappings of a tourist in a new city, tucked away in the side streets and in little neighborhood alcoves are some of the most interesting places you'll be able to chance upon.

Lauded as one of the safest countries to travel, Tokyo will surely live up to its name of being one of the most helpful people in the world. One thing to remember about going to the glitzy city metropolis is, save up well for the trip to experience one heck of a time you won't soon forget. Tokyo is known to be a pretty expensive place to visit. But if you are prepared and you have everything planned well ahead of time, there is no reason not to enjoy the magnificence of the awesome city where there is never a shortage of things to do and find.

There is so much more to this vast and sprawling city metropolis that meets the eye, and definitely goes beyond the typical tourist attractions. Some of the things you will want to keep in mind when visiting Tokyo is how to get information when you need it. Perhaps you need to find out about when the train runs, or when a particular train pulls out of a station. First of all you will find that people from Tokyo will be more than happy to help you but you have to speak English clearly. Locals of Tokyo can generally understand and converse in English but you will have to speak slower than your usual speed and you will have to speak clearly. Do Say "going to" instead of "gonna," say "want to" instead of "wanna."

Important Guidelines

This seems like a given, but, it is a good idea to have the telephone number of your hotel. Should you have any trouble about getting back to the hotel, you can always call and ask directions from where you are and an English speaking receptionist should be able to assist.

If you are coming from the United States then you might want to grab this indispensable, little handy book by Eiji Kanno called "Japan Solo: A Practical Guide for Independent Travelers". This practical handbook is a handy little book covers important information that is written in English and Japanese.

You will be able to find street maps, tips on using the telephone, train schedules and even how to find a toilet. The book is available in Kinokuniya book stores in San Francisco, Los Angeles, and in New York.

You can get in touch with telephone number 212-765-1461 or you may send a letter of inquiry to purchase to 10 West 49th Street, New York 10020. Just to make sure that you cover all bases, have someone write your Tokyo address in kanji for you and keep this on your person for the duration of your stay. Do a bit more of homework and learn a few utilitarian phrases in Japanese.

Mingle and Mix

Pick up some polite Japanese phrases. You wouldn't be expected to respond in Japanese for the duration of the conversation but knowing some of the more polite phrases in Nihongo can take you a long way. You would have by now discovered the willingness and helpfulness of the Japanese people. You can leave your urban defensiveness at home and adapt an openness about you that will be quite refreshing. You will discover that making eye contact in Japan is not at all anything that would constitute threatening.

In fact your smile is the best armory you can carry with you whilst going around the city metropolis. English is a language many people from the cities like to practice; it is a priority for people of all ages. Chat up a local and they may just give you an insider scoop that is not usually found in the tourist books and city information brochure from your hotel.

Heads Up!

You will most likely stumble upon and cross paths with local tourists who are doing as you are; finding their way around the city and heading to possibly one of the same destinations as you are. Strike up a conversation and ask a person from the local tourist group about where they are headed. You will be able to identify these local tourist groups by their flag-carrying leader who usually walks ahead of the bunch. Students are always looking for opportunities to practice their English. You may want to make formal arrangements with a volunteer student. You will also want to grab a phrase book that lists down restaurants and streets. You should also grab hold of a standard guide book that has all the descriptions of the places of interest around Tokyo that gives information on the usual places of popular interest, detailed bits about the principal attractions, admission prices, hours of operation, and how to get there. This can usually be obtained with your hotel concierge.

Worth the Visit!

Just in case you haven't had enough of everything Tokyo, you're right. There is so much more that you will have to do a bit of digging, depending on your interests. Here are just a few more places to hit, that will top off your stay and make your stay well worth every minute.

- Hanayashiki first opened in 1853 and was developed as an amusement park during the industrial revolution of Japan. Imagine the beginnings of this magnificently awesome place that boasts of Japan's oldest roller coaster and Japanese inspired House of Horrors that is surely not one to miss for amusement park enthusiasts. There are kimono and ninja demonstrations and presentations held at the park that is a mesmerizing spectacle to witness. You'll find the park at 2 Chome-28-1 Asakusa Tokyo 111-0032

- Got a stomach for the grotesque? Then the Meguro Parasitological Museum, a museum of oddities founded in 1953, and located on 4-1-1 Shimomeguro, Meguro, Tokyo 153-0064, just might be the place you want to pop into. With fascinatingly morbid and grotesque displays that will boggle the mind and is sure to make a stomach or two turn.

- Hunting down some of the rarest, hard-to-find Japanese books and literature? Jimbocho might just be the place to find that treasure you've been looking for. With miles of transcripts and pages of books, printed vintage materials here are rare finds that collector's dreams are made of. Get lost in midst of ancient texts and manuscripts, retro magazines and books and come alive in the world of written and printed literature.

- Can't get of the day time crowds? Have a taste of the night birds at Piss Alley, or Memory Lane, where quaint, little shanties make up a collection of small backstreet bars and food stalls wafting of meats grilling on a bed hot charcoal. Packed to the hilt almost every night, the air is electric and alive in this dingy thoroughfare that gets its name from its notorious past of being a street of bars with no lavatory facilities, leaving drunks no choice but of relieving themselves right on the street! That is a far cry from what is now, and your bladder will be safely able to get to a toilet on time, just in case. Don't be surprised to find delicacies such as frog sashimi or pig testicles, so, to be on the safe side, follow the crowd for the more usual fare.

- Want a little getaway from the hustle and bustle of the city? One where you can be surrounded by the greenery of nature and reflect without leaving the city too far behind? Head on out to the tranquil quiet sanctuary that is Todoroki Valley, where the word "lush" pales in comparison to the expanse of foliage and fauna is breathtaking as it is magnificent. Situated in the Setagaya ward, the surreal surroundings of the green valley that follows the path of a creek and peppered with quaint and colorful footbridges. Walk amongst the quiet surroundings and arrive at the Fudo Todoroki, a Buddhist temple not too far off from the magical Tatsuzawa Fudo no Taki waterfall. It will be a respite your spirit and soul has sought and should enjoy.

We hope that we have managed to give you a hand in preparing for your trip to Tokyo. Enjoy a magical time as you explore this city metropolis that holds its enigma in the existence and comfortable step of old-world traditions with the modern trappings and conveniences of today's pattern of living. You will surely find the wondrous fascination of how this city, so in tune and aligned with the modern ways of life, manages to capture the richness of their heritage, living in reverence for the past with equal gusto and fervor for the continuity and advancement of society and humans.

PHOTO REFERENCES

Page 1 Photo by user GusbellSStudio via Pixabay.com,

https://pixabay.com/en/tokyo-tower-tokyo-japan-825196/

Page 3 Photo by user Cegoh via Pixabay.com,

https://pixabay.com/en/japan-tokyo-shibuya-japanese-217882/

Page 6 Photo by user Sasint via Pixabay.com,

https://pixabay.com/en/beauty-asia-seductive-pretty-1822520/

Page 11 Photo by user Staffanekstrand via Pixabay.com,

https://pixabay.com/en/japan-tokyo-royal-monastery-wedding-2863792/

Page 12 Photo by user Shbs via Pixabay.com,

https://pixabay.com/en/tokyo-park-nature-japan-asia-2805500/

Page 17 Photo by user xegxef via Pixabay.com,

https://pixabay.com/en/japanese-lantern-lamp-kyoto-2086582/

Page 20 Photo by user StockSnap via Pixabay.com,

https://pixabay.com/en/shibuya-crossing-tokyo-japan-asia-923000/

Page 22 Photo by user Nicolas Raymond via Flickr.com,

https://www.flickr.com/photos/80497449@N04/7378048024/

Page 24 Photo by user hirotomo via Flickr.com,

https://www.flickr.com/photos/travelstar/5921486896/

Page 26 Photo by user Naoki Natsume/ Ishii via Flickr.com,

https://www.flickr.com/photos/gina-rainbow/34185211535/

Page 31 Photo by user 12019 via Pixabay.com,

https://pixabay.com/en/tokyo-japan-city-cities-urban-290980/

Page 35 Photo by user dongpung via Pixabay.com,

https://pixabay.com/en/japan-train-tokyo-931162/

Page 40 Photo by user Jordy Meow via Pixabay.com,

https://pixabay.com/en/ginza-wako-tokyo-architecture-725794/

Page 42 Photo Retrieved from Official Sakura Hotel Website,
https://www.sakura-hotel-hatagaya.com

Page 43 Photo by user J o. via Wikimedia Commons,

https://commons.wikimedia.org/wiki/File:Hotel_Niwa_Toky

o_1F_Lobby_20131028-001.jpg

Page 45 Photo Retrieved from Kevin Frates via KFrates.
Zenfolio.com,

http://kfrates.zenfolio.com/blog/2014/12/tokyo---japan-day-

9-part-3-prince-park-hotel-and-shiba-park

Page 47 Photo Retrieved from Offical Richmond Hotel
Website,
http://asakusa.richmondhotel.jp

Page 49 Photo Retrieved from Andon Website,
http://andon.co.jp

Page 51 Photo Retrieved from H – Rez Website,
http://H-rez.com

Page 53 Photo Retrieved from KNT.co.jp Website,
http://koba.knt.co.jp

Page 55 Photo Retrieved from Cheap Online Hotels Booking
Blog,
http://cheaponlinehotelsbooking.blogspot.com/2015/10/chiyo

da-inn-guest-house-tokyo-japan.html

Page 56 Photo Retrieved from Japan Guidance, https://japanguidance.com/101/best-places-to-stay-in-tokyo-on-a-budget.html

Page 58 Photo Retrieved from Accessible – Japan.com, https://www.accessible-japan.com/hotels/japan/tokyo/adachi/low-range/hotel-coco-grand-kitasenju/

Page 61 Photo by user Ray Chang via Flickr.com,

https://www.flickr.com/photos/jobim1983/761313301/

Page 63 Photo by user Danny O. via Flickr.com,

https://www.flickr.com/photos/dannyboyster/12762879/

Page 65 Photo by user Lou Stejskal via Flickr.com,

https://www.flickr.com/photos/loustejskal/39068630305/

Page 67 Photo by user SteFou via Flickr.com,

https://www.flickr.com/photos/stephen-oung/6264685040/

Page 69 Photo by user S. Yume via Flickr.com,

https://www.flickr.com/photos/syume/5010615129/

Page 71 Photo by user Jeremy Keith via Flickr.com,

https://www.flickr.com/photos/adactio/4501392880/

Page 73 Photo by user Barron Fujimoto via Flickr.com,

https://www.flickr.com/photos/barron/36533684600/

Page 74 Photo by user llee_wu via Flickr.com,

https://www.flickr.com/photos/13523064@N03/14370742691/

Page 76 Photo by user Alpha via Flickr.com,

https://www.flickr.com/photos/avlxyz/28660006/

Page 78 Photo by user Alpha via Flickr.com,

https://www.flickr.com/photos/avlxyz/16010260072/

Page 80 Photo by user Toby Oxborrow via Flickr.com,

https://www.flickr.com/photos/oxborrow/1270576571/

Page 85 Photo by user Toshihiro Gamo via Flickr.com,

https://www.flickr.com/photos/dakiny/16736734861/

Page 87 Photo by user y kawahara via Flickr.com,

https://www.flickr.com/photos/grilledahi/4146826/

Page 90 Photo by user Richard Schneider via Flickr.com,

https://www.flickr.com/photos/picturecorrect/32804126291/

Page 93 Photo by user Daisuke Matsumura via Flickr.com,

https://www.flickr.com/photos/nodoca/33797306/

Page 94 Photo by user nakashi via Flickr.com,

https://www.flickr.com/photos/nakashi/34184797615/

Page 96 Photo by user Olivier Bruchez via Flickr.com,

https://www.flickr.com/photos/bruchez/34247900895/

Page 98 Photo by user Alexandre Gervais via Flickr.com,

https://www.flickr.com/photos/alexgerv/5589368586/

Page 99 Photo by user Naoya Fujii via Flickr.com,

https://www.flickr.com/photos/naoyafujii/3554659488/

Page 101 Photo by user Vasconium via Flickr.com,

https://www.flickr.com/photos/97147533@N02/36672550276/

Page 102 Photo by user nakashi via Flickr.com,

https://www.flickr.com/photos/nakashi/34053490561/

Page 104 Photo by user nakashi via Flickr.com,

https://www.flickr.com/photos/nakashi/29319891682/

Page 108 Photo by user Little Mouse via Pixabay.com,

https://pixabay.com/en/traditional-and-technology-1270519/

Page 109 Photo by user gelli.rosario via Flickr.com,

https://www.flickr.com/photos/130032718@N04/15704908333
/

Page 111 Photo by user e_chaya via Flickr.com,

https://www.flickr.com/photos/e_chaya/5504462218/

Page 113 Photo by user jamesjustin via Flickr.com,

https://www.flickr.com/photos/jamesjustin/2852529200/

Page 115 Photo by user David McKelvey via Flickr.com,

https://www.flickr.com/photos/dgmckelvey/13665076463/

Page 117 Photo by user hiroaki via Flickr.com,

https://www.flickr.com/photos/hwat/104257863/

Page 119 Photo by user aotaro via Flickr.com,

https://www.flickr.com/photos/aotaro/17463375296/

Page 121 Photo by user Geoff Whalan via Flickr.com,
https://www.flickr.com/photos/geoffwhalan/32608663982/

Page 122 Photo by user Alex Chen via Flickr.com,
https://www.flickr.com/photos/wkc1/12023888656/

Page 124 Photo by user Rachel Clarke via Flickr.com,

https://www.flickr.com/photos/rachelc/10152183335/

Page 126 Photo by user Mathieu Thouvenin via Flickr.com,

https://www.flickr.com/photos/mathoov/5280520907/

Page 129 Photo by user marcelokato via Pixabay.com,

https://pixabay.com/en/japan-tokyo-asakusa-japanese-asia-
2638497/

Page 131 Photo by user Aunt Masako via Pixabay.com,

https://pixabay.com/en/meiji-jingu-shrine-dedication-sake-
1665217/

Page 133 Photo by user David Marcos Moreno via
Flickr.com,

https://www.flickr.com/photos/7718047@N08/16424562543/

Page 134 Photo by user aotaro via Flickr.com,

https://www.flickr.com/photos/aotaro/27330689369/

Page 136 Photo by user @arith via Flickr.com,

https://www.flickr.com/photos/arithmatix/35397459196/

Page 137 Photo by user Zengame via Flickr.com,

https://www.flickr.com/photos/zengame/15038606750/

Page 138 Photo by user Gilles Messian via Flickr.com,

https://www.flickr.com/photos/gmessian/34302606056/

Page 140 Photo by user Red-Dream via Flickr.com,

https://www.flickr.com/photos/frf123/27201830714/

Page 142 Photo by user Dana + LeRoy via Flickr.com,

https://www.flickr.com/photos/73601942@N00/380323331/

Page 144 Photo by user Guilhem Vellut via Flickr.com,

https://www.flickr.com/photos/o_0/9114409941/

Page 147 Photo by user judithscharnowski via Pixabay.com,

https://pixabay.com/en/akihabara-tokyo-night-japan-1180397/

Page 148 Photo by user Michael Camplejohn via Flickr.com,

https://www.flickr.com/photos/mcamplejohn/38992745021/

Page 150 Photo by user City Foodsters via Flickr.com,

https://www.flickr.com/photos/cityfoodsters/12403841024/

Page 151 Photo by user James Cridland via Flickr.com,

https://www.flickr.com/photos/jamescridland/4247438362/

Page 153 Photo by user keatl via Flickr.com,

https://www.flickr.com/photos/keatl/11501462595/

Page 155 Photo by user Chris Chen via Flickr.com,

https://www.flickr.com/photos/cchen/5436600944/

Page 157 Photo by user Takayuki Nakagawa via Flickr.com,

https://www.flickr.com/photos/nakagawakun/24046963/

Page 159 Photo by user Melkir via Flickr.com,

https://www.flickr.com/photos/melkir/1835848320/

Page 160 Photo by user jit bag via Flickr.com,

https://www.flickr.com/photos/jitbag/15142774461/

Page 162 Photo by user Kent Wang via Flickr.com,

https://www.flickr.com/photos/kentwang/16228654392/

Page 163 Photo by user Will via Flickr.com,

https://www.flickr.com/photos/infomofo/140891179/

Page 166 Photo by user xegxef via Pixabay.com,

https://pixabay.com/en/asakusa-tokyo-street-travel-japan-2086598/

Page 169 Photo by user sasint via Pixabay.com,

https://pixabay.com/en/beauty-asia-seductive-pretty-1822521/

Page 172 Photo by user derwiki via Pixabay.com,

https://pixabay.com/en/japanese-asia-foliage-ancient-1409839/

REFERENCES

Tokyo Districts – Truly Tokyo

https://trulytokyo.com/tokyo-districts/

Ukiyo – Wikipedia.org

https://en.wikipedia.org/wiki/Ukiyo

Chashitsu – Wikipedia.org

https://en.wikipedia.org/wiki/Chashitsu

Edo Castle – Wikipedia.org

https://en.wikipedia.org/wiki/Edo_Castle

Weather & Seasons – Japan Specialist

https://www.japanspecialist.co.uk/travel-tips/weather-seasons/

Shinkansen – Japan – Guide.com

https://www.japan-guide.com/e/e2018.html

Guide to Tokyo Nightlife: An Introduction – Boutique Japan

https://boutiquejapan.com/tokyo-nightlife-guide/

Roppongi and Akasaka – Truly Tokyo

https://trulytokyo.com/roppongi-and-akasaka/

About Sakura Hotel - Sakura-Hotel-Hatagaya.com

https://www.sakura-hotel-hatagaya.com/

About Richmond Hotel – RichmondHotel.jp

http://asakusa.richmondhotel.jp/

About Green Hotel - GreenHotel.co.jp

http://www.greenhotel.co.jp/en/stay/

Hotel Coco Grand Kita-Senju – Japanican.com

https://www.japanican.com/en/hotel/detail/4018AE3/?ar=13
&sar=130309&gclid=Cj0KCQiAwKvTBRC2ARIsAL0Dgk0jW
e0gKek_LtvD6ACQTfc4FHzN3xplRGRInpNyar7DIoKQXHx
taT8aAq-
_EALw_wcB&gclsrc=aw.ds&dclid=CP2huKip99gCFQ5zjgod
aDYBXg

Dover Street Market in Ginza – DoverStreetMarket.com

http://ginza.doverstreetmarket.com/

Kyubey in Ginza, Tokyo – TheSushiGeek.com

https://www.thesushigeek.com/the-sushi-geek/2016/06/16/kyubey-in-ginza-tokyo

Top 10 places to shop in Tokyo – LonelyPlanet.com

https://www.lonelyplanet.com/japan/tokyo/travel-tips-and-articles/top-10-places-to-shop-in-tokyo/40625c8c-8a11-5710-a052-1479d2776809

Tokyo Shopping Guide – Japan – Guide.com

https://www.japan-guide.com/e/e3053.html

Goodbeer Faucets – **Timeout.com**

https://www.timeout.com/tokyo/bars-and-pubs/goodbeer-faucets

The 38 Essential Tokyo Restaurants: Where to eat ramen, sushi, tempura, and more in Japan's capital – Eater.com

https://www.eater.com/maps/best-tokyo-restaurants

12 Top-Rated Tourist Attractions in Tokyo – PlanetWare.com

http://www.planetware.com/tourist-attractions-/tokyo-jpn-kn-t.htm

The Best Restaurants: Tokyo Top 100 – Timeout.com

https://www.timeout.com/tokyo/restaurants/best-restaurants-tokyo

Feeding Baby
Cynthia Cherry
978-1941070000

Axolotl
Lolly Brown
978-0989658430

Dysautonomia, POTS
Syndrome
Frederick Earlstein
978-0989658485

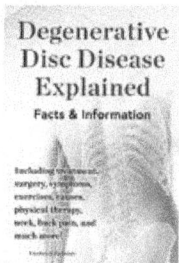

Degenerative Disc
Disease Explained
Frederick Earlstein
978-0989658485

Sinusitis, Hay Fever,
Allergic Rhinitis Explained
Frederick Earlstein
978-1941070024

Wicca
Riley Star
978-1941070130

Zombie Apocalypse
Rex Cutty
978-1941070154

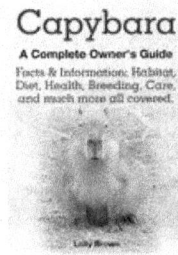

Capybara
Lolly Brown
978-1941070062

Eels As Pets
Lolly Brown
978-1941070167

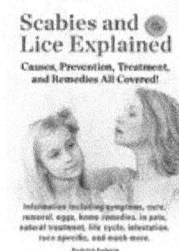

Scabies and Lice Explained
Frederick Earlstein
978-1941070017

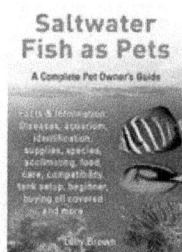

Saltwater Fish As Pets
Lolly Brown
978-0989658461

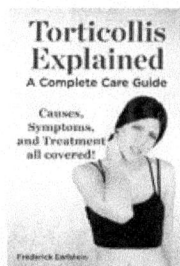

Torticollis Explained
Frederick Earlstein
978-1941070055

Kennel Cough
Lolly Brown
978-0989658409

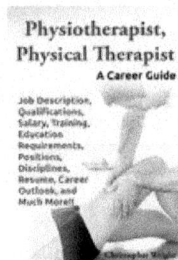

Physiotherapist, Physical
Therapist
Christopher Wright
978-0989658492

Rats, Mice, and Dormice
As Pets
Lolly Brown
978-1941070079

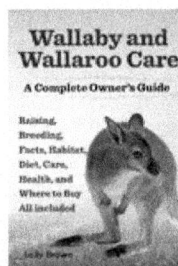

Wallaby and Wallaroo Care
Lolly Brown
978-1941070031

Bodybuilding Supplements
Explained
Jon Shelton
978-1941070239

Demonology
Riley Star
978-19401070314

Pigeon Racing
Lolly Brown
978-1941070307

Dwarf Hamster
Lolly Brown
978-1941070390

Cryptozoology
Rex Cutty
978-1941070406

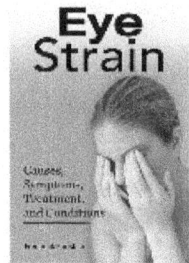

Eye Strain
Frederick Earlstein
978-1941070369

Inez The Miniature Elephant
Asher Ray
978-1941070353

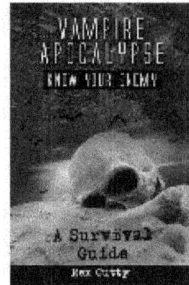

Vampire Apocalypse
Rex Cutty
978-1941070321

www.ingramcontent.com/pod-product-compliance
Lightning Source LLC
Chambersburg PA
CBHW071430090426
42737CB00011B/1616